Chinese Studies in History
FALL-WINTER 1984-85/VOL. XVIII, NO. 1-2

Recent Japanese Studies of
Modern Chinese History

Guest Editor: Joshua A. Fogel
Harvard University

INTRODUCTION

Each year Japan's oldest historical journal, <u>Shigaku</u> <u>zasshi</u>, devotes its May issue to a summary analysis of all the previous year's historical research in Japan. Japanese history occupies the largest space but East Asian history (China, Korea, Southeast Asia, Inner Asia) runs a close second. For the past five years I have been translating two of the subsections from the China section, on Ming-Ch'ing history and on post-Opium War history, for the journal <u>Ch'ing-shih wen-t'i</u>. I owe a great debt of thanks to the editors of that journal-- Sue Naquin, Mary Rankin, and Jim Cole -- for the meticulous care with which they each read at least one draft of every one of my translations.

The Japanese contribution to the study of every area of Chinese history is immense, particularly social and economic history. Equally immense is the annual output of Japanese scholars. It was the original intention of these translations to facilitate the use of Japanese materials by providing in English the same guide the Japanese prepared for themselves every year.

The style of these annual surveys tends to be inordinately turgid, if not simply impenetrable. I have now gone over all the translations that have appeared, <u>completely reedited</u> them, and prepared an index to the articles and a glossary of terms and proper nouns. The notes are intended to facilitate cross referencing from year to year.

Joshua A. Fogel
Harvard University
29 June 1984

MING-CH'ING STUDIES IN JAPAN: 1978

Miki Satoshi, in Shigaku
zasshi 88.5 (May 1979),
220-28.

Ming-Ch'ing historical studies in Japan began in
the postwar period with the common theme of overcoming
the "theory of stagnation." With studies of commodity
production and the landlord system aimed at elucidating
the developmental nature intrinsic to pre-modern society,
studies of peasant struggles that directly trace the independent growth of the small peasant stratum as one of
those developments, and studies of the taxation and
corvée systems that seek the link between the social substructure and the despotic state, a major result has been
a theory of the local gentry aimed at locating their
historical significance over the period of social upheaval from the late Ming through the early Ch'ing. In
the process, a number of essays this year have put forth
views critical of more popular or widely accepted opinions, and raised extremely interesting issues. These
essays are concerned with the basic understanding
needed for a theoretical grasp and overall historical
picture of the Ming-Ch'ing period. They show that we
have reached a turning point from prior Ming-Ch'ing
historical research.

Let us begin with agricultural management and the
land system. In 1976, Adachi Keiji (along with Shimasue
Kazuyasu) proposed the theoretical construct of a "state
serf system" for Ming-Ch'ing society. This year Adachi
published two articles on agricultural management in
which he develops this idea empirically: "Agricultural

Management in the Late Ming and Early Ch'ing: A Reevaluation of the Shen-shih nung-shu"[a] (Shirin 61.1), and
"The Circulation of Soybean Meal Fertilizer and Commercial Agriculture in the Ch'ing"[b] (Tōyōshi kenkyū 37.3).
The former evaluates what is described in the Shen-shih
nung-shu as landlord management (hereafter, "Shen-style
management") to be "rich peasant management" with the developmental capacity of the petit bourgeoisie; Kojima
Kazuo had denied such a developmental nature. Adachi
investigates "Shen-style management" from the two perspectives of technology and management. On the technology side, "Shen-style management" developed intensive
small farming methods such as massive investments in
fertilizers, deep furrowing with such hand tools as the
iron cramp (t'ieh-ta), and a high degree of investment
in short-term labor, and it was deeply involved in commercial agriculture. Thus, Mr. Shen reached a "stage
of high-level, small-scale commodity production" by
planning for increased labor productivity (such as labor-
saving methods in fertilizing) and aimed as even greater
profits. Furthermore, Adachi sets the operating standards of "Shen-style management" at approximately forty
mou (Kojima had said ten-odd mou) and supports his developmental position with calculations of operating income
and expenditures. His arguments drawn from a thorough
immersion in the Shen-shih nung-shu are persuasive. However, on the expenditure side of his calculations, Adachi
carefully considers taxes, but does not analyze labor
requirements. During this period in the Kiangnan region, the equitable field-equitable labor system was in
effect. The downfall of chung-jen (middle and small
landlords with special privileges) because of corvée
burdens became a major social problem. The decline of
these chung-jen landlords and the rosy picture of "Shen-
style management" [i.e., landlord management] are con-
spicuously symmetrical. How to transcend this discrepancy

[as to whether landlords were really declining--JAF] remains a problem.

The second article investigates the growth and
changes throughout the Ch'ing dynasty in the circulation of soybean meal fertilizer, the main fertilizer in
Kiangnan during the period, and of its source, the soybean, as an index to the social expansion of rich peasant management. According to Adachi, a structure of
distribution with soybeans and soybean meal fertilizer
as a "first-class commodity" came into existence in the
mid-Ch'ing. It had three traits: 1) agriculture using
soybean meal fertilizer and reaching the "stage of high-
level, small-scale commodity production" was widely
established; 2) the development of Kiangnan's agriculture brought about a nation-wide market for the fertilizer produced in the Northwest; and 3) the increase in
the level of productivity brought about by soybean meal
fertilizer made even "impoverished peasants" inclined
to use it. However, because of changes in the conditions
of distribution in the late Ch'ing (such as the introduction of Western goods and an increase in likin extractions), rich peasant management was forced into an
"across-the-board regression." In this regard, Adachi
sees the establishment of a managerial viewpoint held
by the "upper" or "rich" peasants (shang-nung, fu-nung,
shang-hu) a viewpoint which for Ch'ing period Kiangnan
was based on: (a) the large size of surface area being
managed (not the amount of land owned); (b) the use of
hired labor; and (c) the use of fertilizers for high
labor productivity. But, especially in the case of
(a), in Adachi's sources (cf. Wen-sheng) "upper peasant"
(shang-nung) and "upper household" (shang-hu) are terms
used to make distinctions within the tenant stratum,
whereas "rich peasant" (fu-nung) is contrasted with
"tenant," unable to use hired labor and relying on
"companion labor" (cf. Tao-ch'ing chen chih, Ch'ien-

lung edition). And when we consider management, must we
not differentiate clearly, also, between the landlords
and the tenants (who had half of their harvest expropri-
ated)? In the case of tenants, it is doubtful whether
(b) and (c) were readily pertinent even to the shang-
nung among them; and it seems that the use of soybean
meal fertilizer, Adachi's (c), is quite an important
element in this regard.

   Kawakatsu Mamoru's essay, still in progress, "Cotton Production and Water Utilization in the Yangtze
Delta, Late Ming to Early Ch'ing (1)"[a] (Kyūshū daigaku
Tōyōshi ronshū 6), is concerned with clarifying the link
between cotton production and the land system. In this
first part, he describes the antagonistic relationship
between tenants who persisted in cotton production and
landlords who urged conversion to rice production. The
confrontation was between tenants, who benefited from
paying rent in a fixed amount in kind, and landlords,
who had to acquire rice to fulfill state extractions
and white rice for imperial use and who were hamstrung
by their relationship with commercial capital which controlled the process of conversion between rice and
cotton. He argues that the "peculiar situation" of
the late Ch'ung-chen years (1628-44) is reflected
herein. Furthermore, Kawakatsu relates (citing the
Ch'i-chen chi-wen lu) that at this time a rent in wheat
became the rule in Soochow and "continued thereafter
until the 19th and 20th centuries." This needs to be
reconciled with Amano Motonosuke's view that rent paid
in wheat did not exist as a usual practice in the
Kiangnan delta. Kawakatsu's citation speaks to a symmetrical situation when "rice production was insuffi-
cient and winter wheat was harvested in abundance." In
fact, this "peculiar situation" existed for only an
extremely short period of time [as evidenced by a citation from the same Ch'i-chen chi-wen lu--JAF]: "For

the past several years, arable land has been planted but
has gone to waste; for each mou, a tou of wheat is demanded in rent, and they really cannot afford it."

    Kusano Yasushi (in his essay, "Deterioration of
Rice Fields in the Late Ming-Early Ch'ing: The Case of
the Sand Flats in the Lower Yangtze Delta,"[a] Hōbun ronsō
41) analyzes the decline during the late Ming to early
Ch'ing of customary rice paddy practices widespread from
the Sung and Yüan. Specifically he looks at the transition from the mai-chia ch'eng-chia[1] system to a system
of obligatory rent deposit (ya-tsu)--this change also
represented a degeneration away from the kuo-t'ou[2] system). He claims that this deterioration was mediated
by the colonization of the sand flats by "powerful landowners" (t'u-hao) and "embankment overseers" (yü-t'ou)
and later by contracted tenants. Kusano makes free use
of the various editions of the Ch'ung-ming hsien chih
for the K'ang-hsi, Ch'ien-lung, Kuang-hsu, and Republican periods, but each of his arguments lacks clarity.
Let us take up several doubtful points. 1) The actual
nature of the "powerful landowners and embankment overseers" remains unclear. The source which mentions their
first appearance is the record of a tenant who had re-
sisted rent payment (wan-tien); and this contradicts
Kusano's conclusion where he speaks of "those embankment overseers and contracted tenants of the powerful
landowning gentry class." 2) Kusano believes that
colonization costs in the sand flats were consistently
footed by the tenants; but, how then do we understand
statements such as "'landlords themselves paid to have
dikes constructed'" and "'allocate payment according to
the size of one's landholding'" which appear in the Li-
p'ai kung-chu chih of the Ch'ien-lung period? Furthermore, the link between systems of sand flat colonization
and landlord-tenant relations should be made clear. One
cannot but feel that on the whole Kusano's grand concep-

tual scheme has preceded his evidence.

In the past, studies in social and economic history linked various phenomena to theories of stages of development or theories of economic structure, but investigations of the "concrete economic background" that brought about these phenomena remained incomplete. With this in mind, Nakayama Mio ("Secular Trends in Rice Prices in Kiangnan During the Early Ch'ing,"[a] Shigaku zasshi 87.9) pioneers in the field of commodity price history as an effective means to clarify the overall picture of economic fluctuations. She analyzes with precision the utility of the history of pre-modern commodity prices, rejects statistical techniques based solely on numbers as a research method, and advocates grasping the trends in commodity prices through the numerous writings of contemporaries that reveal how they actually felt. In this piece, she traces closely the trend in rice prices from the late Wan-li reign until the mid-Ch'ien-lung period. She points out that the rise and fall of rice prices was not simply the result of natural phenomena but was tied into the booms and slumps of overall economic activity.

Two articles concerned with village "community" (kyōdōtai) deal with lands protected by embankments in Kiangnan: Hamashima Atsutoshi, "Irrigation Practices in the Kiangnan Delta in the First Half of the Ming: A Reinvestigation of the T'ien-t'ou System"[a] (Shichō N.S. 3) and Tsurumi Naohiro, "Several Problems Concerning "Community" in China of Old: The Kiangnan Delta Region in the Ming and Ch'ing"[a] (Shichō N.S. 4). Hamashima's essay discusses in detail the t'ien-t'ou system by which is meant the customary practices of repairing embankments and dredging creeks. Concretely, by centering his discussion on Yao Wen-hao's Hsiu-chu yü-t'an shih-i (extremely detailed regulations concerning the t'ien-t'ou system during the Hung-chih reign), he explains the

political process surrounding water control at that time
and gets at the actual state of affairs concerning local
cultivator-landlords' domination of water control, a
community usufruct. According to Hamashima, Yao Wen-
hao's t'ien-t'ou system codified customary practices pre-
supposing local gentry "village control" amidst a decline
in water control techniques that accompanied an earlier
loosening of relations within the village; the t'ien-t'ou
system represented a "reorganization within a mold." On
the basis of the Chiao-min pang-wen (which gave li-lao-
jen and li-chang various powers including jurisprudential
authority), he also concludes that local landlord "control" included "official protection against outside
forces" and extended to their own tenants as well as
self-cultivator peasants. The existence of powerful
"control" by landlords in the early Ming urges a study of
the establishment of "gentry control"[3] from the late Ming
on.

Tsurumi's essay sets up as the "basis of social regeneration" (cf. Marx's letter to [Vera] Zasulich) a
distinctly Chinese kyōdōtai which "by virtue of its being
preserved continued as the object of exploitation while
the process of 'modernization' progressed." He tries to
see it as something which advanced the development from
socialist land reform in China to the people's communes.
In concrete terms, he limits his discussion of the
kyōdōtai to its functions. In its connection to the
li-chia system, he investigates: (1) communal work in
water control (wet land cultivation based on landlord
control over communal regulations); (2) mutual aid communal work in farming (the companion labor [pan-kung]
and exchange labor [huan-kung] that were common among
poor peasantry); and (3) communal religious beliefs and
festivals. Tsurumi points out that past studies, including his own, have emphasized only the control side of
the li-chia system. He tries to see the side in which

the communal work of the poorer peasants sustained their own existence, gave birth to small peasant mutual solidarity, and developed into a "struggle for independence and stability" (such as the rent resistance movements developing from li-chia and embankment work linkages). Tsurumi's article makes a great contribution to the advancement of Chinese kyōdōtai theory in attempting to see clearly the emergence of socialist reform from the pre-modern Chinese kyōdōtai. On this point, we must analyze in detail how within the kyōdōtai the small peasantry was bound together by a dual cohesion between (1) and (2) (communal work along the embankments), on the one hand, and even more tightly knit because of (3) (communal religious ceremonies), on the other; and how the landlord's rule was integrated with the solidarity and "regeneration" of the small peasantry. Hamashima's point that the logic of cohesion due to embankment connections in the anti-rent movement does not accord directly with with li-chia connections along the embankments is important ("for the reorganization of water control practices in the Kiangnan delta in the late Ming and early Ch'ing").

In his essay, "On the Nature of Chinese Feudalism: The Ming Li-chia System"[a] (Okayama daigaku hōgakkai zasshi 26.2), Iwama Kazuo seeks to clarify the structural linkage between the li-chia system and landlord control through the distinctly Chinese "feudal village." The main subject of this piece, however, is the system itself which reflected the actual state of affairs (i.e., the landlord system) under Chinese feudalism. It was this system which Chu Yuan-chang, creator of the li-chia system, confronted. Iwama argues that the li-chia system was based on a complex "feudal village" with two levels of "cooperation" which were disguised by landlord control: (a) a rural, local geographic "cooperation" and (b) a supra-village "cooperation" as seen in the ch'i-chuang-hu[4] (although (a) was the basis of li-chia organization). Criticizing Tsurumi's theory of the solitary

household and Kuribayashi Nobuo's basic centers of population theory, Iwama indicates that the essence of the
system was: (1) tenants were, ideally, included among the
li-chia members, and (2) li-chia organization was not
necessarily based on the local geographic village. On
the other hand, the decline of the li-chia system was a
dissolution of (1) because of the development of supra-
village landownership (i.e., (2)). Also, there were a
series of reforms through the late Ming aimed at a reorganization of (1) and an amelioration of any opposition between (1) and (2). Iwama argues that through
this process the village took on a feudal character or
"dual fictitious blood ties." His innovative conception
of the li-chia system from his perspective on the "feudal
village" contradicts our past understanding of the li-
chia system. While (1) in particular seems to be central
to Iwama's idea, he explicitly states that li-chia constituents were "responsible for corvée." This would imply
equitable labor requirements in which the tenant farmers
bore corvée duties. However, tenant farmers did corvée
in place of landlords. Furthermore, the corvée they performed which was predicated on "personal and status relations" between landlords and tenants[5] and proper li-chia
corvée (which was a function of "taxation" and re-produc-
tion) cannot be seen in the same light.
     Okuzaki Yūji's Chūgoku kyōshin jinushi no kenkyū[a]
should be cited first in the category of "theories of
the gentry" which became the main theme of Ming-Ch'ing
studies in the 1970's. This major work aims at an overall understanding of authority in the Ming-Ch'ing period
from an analysis of gentry-landlord thought (defined as
"the points of contact in the everyday intellectual
struggle between the rulers and the ruled"). He centers
his discussion on the Yüan family of Chia-shan county in
Chekiang. Also, the author suggests a periodization of
knowledge that classifies the late Ming-early Ch'ing as

the late feudal period. I can neither adequately introduce nor evaluate the whole of this book, and I would
prefer to leave these details to Noguchi Tetsurō's book
review which appeared in Kindai Chūgoku (#5).

Wada Masashiro has written two essays concerned with
the social position of chü-jen as a distinct stratum
within the larger gentry body: "A Study of the Formative
Process of the Chü-jen Class in the Ming: An Investigation of Examination System Regulations,"[a] Shigaku
zasshi 87.3; "The Development of the Ordinance ōn the
Privilege of Exemption from Labor Service and the Legal
Status of Chü-jen in the Late Ming,"[b] Tōyō gakuhō 60.1-2.
In the first essay, he discusses how chü-jen (those who
had failed the metropolitan examinations), who from the
early Ming had been compelled to enter the National University, later from the Hsuan-te and Cheng-t'ung reigns
(i.e., from 1426 on) took up residence in the countryside and held a definite social position in rural society.
The state, however, regulated them by the repeated pro-
mulgation of examination system regulations (which set a
limit on the number of times a person could sit for the
metropolitan exams). Finally in 1595 government policy
changed to publicly recognize chü-jen living in the
countryside in an announcement of "recommendation and
examination regulations."

The second essay analyzes the changes in the standard amount of corvée exemption in the privileged exemption (or yu-mien, ordinance and its practical regulations. These appeared in the process of corvée reform
from the equitable corvée laws of the Cheng-t'ung years
(1436-49) to the equitable field-equitable labor system
of the Wan-li reign (1573-1619). Thus, in the various
regulations beginning with the 1494 yu-mien ordinance
(when chü-jen were first exempted) and continuing through
the "rules" of 1555 which aimed at limiting yu-mien (as
well as the rules of 1586 which regulated the amount of

chün-t'ien), the chü-jen held a position below all ranked
officials, on the same level as sheng-yüan and chien-
sheng. In short, they were rather coldly treated. However, "a status distinction based on differences of background in the examinations and schools" (a difference
between chin-shih and chü-jen on the one hand and between
chu-jen and sheng-yüan/chien-sheng on the other) became
clear in the regulations under the equitable field-
equitable labor system. Wada says that this change
clarified the position of the chü-jen, who appeared on
the scene in late Ming society as the principal object
of corvée legal reform. This solidly empirical essay
elucidates the rise of chü-jen as a new stratum within
the ruling class from the perspective of the examination
system and yu-mien privilege that established gentry
status, and it provides a firm advance in gentry theory.

Concrete studies of the inner working of the corvée
system, aside from Wada's work, were published in 1978.
Hoshi Ayao (in "A Study of Chin-hua-yin,"[c] Yamagata
daigaku kiyō 9.1) reinvestigates chin-hua-yin (Gold-
Floral-Silver) about which Shimizu Taiji and Horii
Kazuo have held different opinions, and he clarifies
its origin and nature. Hoshi argues that it was first
institutionalized in 1433.[6] Furthermore, it was qualitatively different from the che-liang-yin[7] which was
effected in 1436. Later, during the process of conversion to che-liang-yin, a substantial insufficiency
caused by the fixing of quotas and the rate of com-
mutation caused a permanent surcharge to be levied on
rice and wheat payable in silver, and also caused silver to be borrowed constantly for border troop provisions.

Iwami Hiroshi, in his "An Historical Source on the
Chün-yao-fa"[a] (in Uchida ronshū), introduces a new
historical source on the equitable corvée law in its
early period (1433 through the early 1460's), and

expresses doubt about the common view that equitable
labor service was enforced in this early period.

Meguro Katsuhiko (in his essay, "A Look at the
Shun-chuang-fa in Chekiang During the Yung-cheng Reign,"[a]
Rekishi kenkyū, Aichi Kyōika University, 24) tries to
understand the shun-chuang-fa[8] not merely as an institution within the corvée structure but as an institution
intended for integration into the pao-chia system. Taking the example of Chia-hsiang prefecture in Chekiang,
he largely confirms past theories. Meguro concludes
that the shun-chuang-fa aimed at rationalization by
doing away with the complexities caused by the coexist-
ence of the li-chia and pao-chia systems within a village. But this is only one aspect, and the historical
nature of the shun-chuang-fa does not become clear in
this piece. Moreover, reliance on a supra-historical
phenomenon like "confusion in customs and public order"
to account for integration of the shun-chuang-fa and
pao-chia in the Yung-cheng period is unpersuasive. What
we need is a structural elucidation of the link between
the enforcement of the pao-chia system and the reform
of the corvée system from the late Ming.

Kuribayashi Nobuo's essay, "Rural Administration
in the Early Ch'ing"[a] (Shakai bunka shigaku 15), analyzes the functions (levying taxes, population control,
law and order, etc.) of village "administration" as
seen in the connections between the li-chia/pao-chia
and the ti-fang, hsiang-pao, and ti-pao. He considers
that there was a transition in the structure of "village
adminstration" from "corvée-style autonomy abetting
official control" to a "broad administrative network
of official control."

This past year saw a number of essays in the field
of the history of popular uprisings that interpreted
the rebellions from the Ming-Ch'ing transition through
the Taipings as an historically linked process of

development. Mori Masao's essay, "The Present State and
Problems in Historical Studies of Popular Rebellions:
A Rejoinder to Kobayashi Kazumi"[c] (in Kōza, vol. 1),
begins by asking how we can transcend and then integrate
the gulf between the logic of pre-modern and of modern
history. After analyzing the views first of Kobayashi
Kazumi and then Sōda Hiroshi, Hamashima Atsutoshi,
Tanaka Masatoshi, Yokoyama Suguru, Sano Manabu, Suzuki
Chūsei, Yasuno Shōzō, and Kojima Shinji, he presents
the following noteworthy views. (1) In the 17th
century, the "most widespread" class struggles in south
and central China were nu-pien[8]; rent resistance movements were of a "secondary" nature. Thus, amid the
"manifoldly blended and stratified social relations,"
the master-nu-p'u relationship was the "weakest rung."
In contrast, the landlord-tenant relationship was the
only organizational essential in the various social
relations which "still retained a firm vitality."
(2) In the 18th century, we see for the first time "a
rent resistance current becoming widespread." In the
first half of the 19th century, "'quantitative changes'
that prepared rent resistance uprisings for making
'qualitative changes' were firmly underway." Mori also
reminds us that in the process of "quantitative change"
the people themselves caused the nurturing and development of "revolutionary conditions" at the level of
"qualitative change." In particular, his first point
(1) differs from the common view (that considers the
rent resistance movement to be the fundamental class
struggle of that time), and we hope that Mori will
pursue further the empirical work he has already begun
(published in 1977). Yet, while he considers the "17th
century as the period of greatest nationwide revolts
which occurred at the end" of pre-modern times, he
lacks a perspective on peasant rebellions in north
China. It is necessary to have a comprehensive grasp

on south and central China as well as north China.
This is because even for the Kiangnan gentry landlord
class, uprisings in north China appeared as an immense
threat and became an essential element to their sense
of crisis.

Mori has also written on rebellions in the Fukien-
Kwangtung-Kiangsi border regions where in the 17th
century rent resistance uprisings were exceptionally
"concentrated" ("Huang T'ung's Rent Resistance Uprising
in Ning-hua County, Fukien, in the 17th Century (Part
3),"[d] Nagoya daigaku bungakubu kenkyū ronshū 74). Investigating the rebellion of Huang T'ung from many
angles, this third part addresses rent resistance
uprisings in Kiangsi. At the center of the uprisings
in Kiangsi as well were armed bands of tenants known
as t'ien-ping or t'ien-tsei. However, many Kiangsi
tenants were migrants, k'o-min or k'o-hu, so relations
between landlords (native locals) and tenants were
governed by the general landlord-tenant contradiction
as well as a native-migrant contradiction. Furthermore, migrant people's organizations, known as k'o-
kang, played a specific role in the organization and
activities of t'ien-ping. Thus, Mori argues, rent
resistance uprisings were comprehensive class struggles
caused by t'ien-ping, k'o-min, or k'o-kang who were
outside the local social order.

Nishimura Kazuyo ("On Nu-p'u in the Ming and
Ch'ing,"[a] Tōyōshi kenkyū 36.4) reviews past scholarship on nu-p'u who were the main actors in the nu-pien
and raises issues for future research. She argues
that we should investigate inclusively the manifold
living and work situations of nu-p'u when we set up
historical categories for them; and we should pay particular attention to the hao-nu as a central group
within the Ming-Ch'ing nu-p'u stratum. This point
applies as well to the nu-pien. Thus, Nishimura says,

the organizational and developmental character of nu-
pien reflect the role played by hao-nu who held a "broad
perspective"; and at the same time their role gave a
complexity and fragility to the nu-pien. However,
while regarding the hao-nu as the "detonators of 'natural nu-pien'" she does not make clear when those
opportune moments for hao-nu themselves to rise up
would occur. Furthermore, can we say that within the
contradiction inherent in the master-nu-p'u relationship the contradiction between masters and hao-nu was
primary?

In his essay, "Pirates Along the Sea Near Lingnan
and the Rebellion of Yüeh Kang and the Twenty-Four
Generals"[a] (Aoyama shigaku 5), Sakuma Shigeo criticizes
Katayama Seijirō's thesis on the pirate rebellions (as
class struggles by middle and lower merchants). He
indicates the wide range of class backgrounds of the
pirates, and reevaluates the rebellion of Yueh Kang as
"a local bandit rebellion."

On religious organizations and religious rebellions, such as the White Lotus Sect, Noguchi Tetsurō
(in "Introduction to the Study of the History of
Chinese Religious Societies: Trends in the Study of
the History of the White Lotus Sect,"[e] Kindai Chūgoku 4)
reviews a plethora of past theories from a variety of
perspectives, making this essay extremely useful for
future research.

Asai Motoi (in "Historical Sources for the Rebellion of Hsü Hung-ju in the Late Ming,"[a] Tōyō gakuhō
60.1-2) organizes and classifies historical sources
relating to Hsü's rebellion. Asai introduces new
material he discovered on those responsible for crushing the rebellion, and he hopes to develop some new
ideas on rebellion in the future.

Yasuno Shōzō's "Yen Ju-i and the White Lotus
Rebellion"[a] (in Namae ronshū) tells the story of Yen

Ju-i who was active as a local Shensi official in putting down the White Lotus Rebellion in the Chia-ch'ing
years, and later wrote the San-sheng pien-fang pei-lan.
    On popular religion aside from the White Lotus
Sect, there is Suzuki Chūsei's "The Ta-ch'eng Sect of
Chang Pao-t'ai in Yunnan in the Mid-Ch'ing"[a] (Tōyōshi
kenkyū 36.4). Suzuki analyzes the doctrinal content
and the circumstances of the founding period, and the
changes in the organizational activities of this sect
which had spread from various Yangtze delta provinces
as far as Chihli and was officially repressed in 1746.
Suzuki also provides a diagram of how the group, which
possessed a strict doctrine prescribing their boundaries, changed into a collection of small bands after
their founder's death and how "the route to improvement and purification" of the religion was closed off
amidst extreme infighting.
    In the field of political history, there were
three essays on the early Ming. Taniguchi Kikuo's "On
the State of 'Ta-hsia' of Ming Yü-chen"[a] (in Uchida
ronshū) investigates the state of Ta-hsia, founded in
Szechwan in the late Yüan-early Ming period. Although
religion in Ta-hsia was based on belief in the Maitreya
these religious views never became the state's ruling
principle; the social structure remained as before,
"Confucian and traditional." The result was that
despite the Maitreya belief which served as the bond
for Ming Yü-chen's group, they sought a compromise
with indigenous powers (e.g., by acknowledging landlord control) before facing the problem of setting up a
political structure in Szechwan.
    Danjō Hiroshi ("The Establishment of the Ming
Dynasty: The Impeachment Cases of the Hung-wu Reign
and the Relocation of the Capital,"[a] Tōyōshi kenkyū
37.3) brilliantly examines the process by which the
Hung-wu Emperor, who had begun his reign with his

"Southerners' regime," sought to extricate himself from
a closed administration in order to "bring about the
unification of the realm." Danjō regards this as part
of a continuous process by which the Ming state from
Hung-wu to Yung-lo established itself (the intervening
Chien-wen reign "being a period of temporary reversal")
contrary to the commonly held view that there was a
definite break between the Hung-wu and Yung-lo regimes.
In concrete terms, he clarifies the organic linkages
between the five impeachment cases (including the cases
of K'ung Yin and Kuo Huan that have not previously been
researched) and the issue of the moving of the capital
on the one hand, and the string of reforms in the
central bureaucracy and local society including the
establishment of the "six boards of the system of pu-
cheng shih-ssu," the enforcement of the li-chia system,
the overhauling of the bureaucratic structure, and the
enactment of the policies of population deportation and
the enfeoffment of princes. He argues that the final
maneuver of the regime in the early Ming was Yung-lo's
moving the capital to Peking in 1421.

In his piece, "The Policies of the Chien-wen
Emperor"[a] (Jimbun ronkyū, Kansai Gakuin University,
27.4), Sakakura Atsuhide treats the second Ming emperor
from the same perspective as Danjō. According to Sakakura, the Chien-wen Emperor who acceded to the throne
under the system of princely enfeoffment did not continue the late Hung-wu structure, attempted to establish
his own system based in the South, and carried out policies determined to cut out of power the princes who
threatened his imperial might.

On early Ch'ing politics and thought, Ōtani
Toshio has written "The Political Background to the
Conviction of Tai Ming-shih: The Connection Between
the Schools of Tai Ming-shih and Fang Pao"[a] (Shirin
61.4). Ōtani charts the different "intellectual

travels" of Tai Ming-shih (devotée of the statecraft school
historical research) and Fang Pao (follower of the Sung
school), both of hermit backgrounds. He looks at them
in light of the tendencies for Han Chinese to become
bureaucrats or to remain local scholars in the overall
intellectual climate at the time of the case involving
Tai Ming-shih in 1711. This case he considers the
turning point from tolerance to severity in Ch'ing rule
over Han Chinese.

In the field of intellectual history, Mizoguchi
Yūzō has written a comprehensive and dynamic essay linking late Ming politics, society, and economics with the
thought of the Tung-lin faction: "The Thought of the
'Tung-lin Faction': The Development of Chinese Thought
in the Pre-modern Period (Part 1)"[a] (Tōyō bunka kenkyūjo
kiyō 75). Mizoguchi rejects our past simplistic understanding of the Tung-lin (intellectually opposed to the
wu-shan wu-o clique, politically opposed to the Grand
Secretariat, and economically consisting of middle and
small landlords). He regards the "thought of Tung-lin
scholars" as an "intellectual current of men" who
sought common reforms and "were groping for a new
structure and morality" during the politically and
economically violent era of the late Ming. Thus, the
Tung-lin faction was a new political force, which
opposed the "sole despotic rule of the Emperor" in the
central bureaucracy and sought a new political structure based on landlord hegemony. In the countryside,
as the "main body of the landlord class" (without any
quantitative concepts of big, middle, or small), they
sought stability and a strengthening of the overall
landlord system (they opposed hao-ch'iang, who opened
the way to large-scale gentry landholdings, but they
also supported the suppression of popular uprisings
and nu-pien against these hao-ch'iang). In concrete
terms, Mizoguchi regards the late Ming political process

as a struggle between "state hegemony" (the Emperor and
eunuch cliques) and "local hegemony" (the Tung-lin
faction). He considers the thoughts and activities of
Ch'en Lung-cheng of Chia-shan county in Chekiang as the
essence of local "yu-ts'un hegemony," and as typical of
the "main body of the landlords" who adhered to local
realities.

Mizoguchi raises extremely broad issues. (1) In
terms of political thought, the Tung-lin faction advocated "monarchy with public rights and public rule."
With respect to the imperial institution, this kung
(public) in actuality urged a recognition of the ssu
(private, the economic reality) of the "main body of the
landlord class." It also locally sought a societal
chün (egalitarianism) by controlling the hao-ch'iang.
(2) In the area of social thought, they called for
the promotion of agriculture. (3) In philosophical
thought, they sought a "harmony of social hierarchy."
Furthermore, Mizoguchi proposes that the principal
contradition of the time was not landlords vs. tenants
and nu-p'u but the state vs. landlords and tenants.
This theory of the Tung-lin faction is constructed
on the basis of the voluminous collected writings of
Tung-lin scholars. He then proceeds to the construction of a comprehensive historical picture of the late
Ming that is profoundly sophisticated.

Ōtani Toshio's piece, "Research Notes in Ch'ing
Intellectual History: On Mizoguchi Yūzō's Argument"[6]
(Atarashii rekishigaku no tame ni 152), tries to establish "points from which to grasp Ch'ing intellectual
history as a whole." He suggests the small-scale
management thesis of Adachi Keiji with respect to
"socio-economic knowledge" as a foundation on which
to construct an intellectual history, and proposes the
formulation of "thought which reflected the rich farmer
consciousness" of "local scholars among the people"

during the Ch'ing. However, how then are we to understand the connection with the thought of the Tung-lin
faction which, as Mizoguchi has clearly shown, was
thoroughly in accord with the landlord class?

Finally, in the volume Hoshi ronshū, there are
thirteen essays concerned with Ming-Ch'ing history.
These include: Kawakatsu Mamoru, "A Rebellion of
Nanking Troops in the Late Ming: A Sketch of the Late
Ming Urban Structure,"[b] which stresses the role of out-
laws in popular uprisings; Yamane Yukio, "Brokers in
North China Markets in the Ming-Ch'ing"[a] which clarifies gentry (particularly sheng-yüan and chien-sheng)
control of markets; and Oyama Masaaki, "On Hired Labor
Laws in the Ming-Ch'ing Era"[a] which traces the links
between the revision of the Hired Labor Laws and the
independence of small farmers. I have reviewed the
contents of this volume in detail in Tōyō gakuhō
60.1-2.

I am able to introduce only an extremely small
part of the more than sixty essays concerning the Ming-
Ch'ing period published in 1978. I apologize for
reluctantly having to leave out many important articles.

MING-CH'ING STUDIES IN JAPAN: 1979
Fuma Susumu, in Shigaku
zasshi 89.5 (May 1980),
205-11.

The publishing world and the world of historical
scholarship in China are showing great activity at present. Books such as the Ch'en-ch'ueh chi which Japanese scholars have rarely seen are being revised and
published; Ch'ing-shih lun-ts'ung (Symposium on Chinese
history) has begun publication and is full of solid
research. Inscriptional materials of various kinds have
been and will continue to be published. Furthermore,
little by little the ice is being broken for meaningful
exchange between Japanese and Chinese scholars who work
in the history of the Ming-Ch'ing period. Clearly this
tendency will flourish in the future.

In Japan, on the other hand, European and Japanese
historical studies are now stressing "social history."
We do not yet have a precise theory about just what sort
of history "social history" is. But, having, for the
present, freed itself from simplistic economic deter-
minism and not concerned only with class relations, it
apparently aims to delve also into popular consciousness
and lifestyles. Thus, it has become a necessary and
welcome direction to pursue. For nearly a decade in
the field of Ming-Ch'ing history, "gentry theory,"
which has dealt with the problem of large-scale gentry
land ownership, occupied the mainstream of discussion,
oblivious to the trends in the study of European and
Japanese history.[1] However, even hothouse-variety Ming-
Ch'ing historical research is without a doubt now
approaching a turning point.

The most straightforward explanation of this tendency appears in an essay by Mori Masao, "Disruptions
in the Social Order in the Late Ming"[e] (in Nagoya

ronshū). In 1977, Mori published his "The Uprising of
the Wu-lung hui in Sha-ch'i, T'ai-ts'ang Prefecture, in
1645"[f] (in Nakayama ronsō). In that article he gave a
practical demonstration of how, by avoiding a methodology which gives pat explanations based on the conventional wisdom, socio-economic history was in the process
of turning a sharp corner. His latest article criticizes more explicitly the methods used in Ming-Ch'ing
socio-economic history since World War II. Yet Mori
does not conclude merely with a critique. He addresses
the concrete problem of what this disruption of order
in the late Ming entailed, and he investigates it on the
basis of selections from the feng-su sections of local
gazetteers. According to Mori, the disorder of the
late Ming was a disruption in all social relations:
high and low status, regular commoner-déclassé, old-
young, superior-inferior, landlord-tenant, master-
servant, gentry-commoner, etc. His main points are
as follows: (1) The phenomenon of the overturning of
the social order cannot be understood by mechanically
applying the concept of landlord-tenant relations as
an economic category. He criticizes this practice,
which until now has concentrated on the rent resistance
movement, a result of the landlord-tenant relationship,
and which has cut it off from other upheavals. (2) In
addition to vertical class and status relations in local
society, there were communal relations along horizontal
lines which had a preeminently spiritual quality. This
point transcends the particular exploitation of labor
inherent in the master-bondservant relationship, and
suggests the existence of a relationship between the
established constituents of a community (the respect-
able commoners) and the discriminated-against quasi-
constituents (the nu-p'u). (3) The position of the
gentry and literati in local society was comparatively
declining. This point poses a frontal attack on

"gentry theory" from the work of the late Shigeta
Atsushi on, which held that "gentry control" was established in the late Ming-early Ch'ing period.

Mori's criticism is severe. Scholars who have
hitherto sought to reduce all phenomena to relations of
production, and moreover scholars who, even while
attaching conditions, understand the landlord-tenant
relationship to be the primary relation of production
and try to explain all phenomena deductively from it,
will have to respond to Mori's critique. Mori does not
draw any hasty conclusions. But there is a need to per-
sist in putting that age-old question both to Mori and
to ourselves: What happened after the late Ming (which
he cites for its disruptions in the social order)? And
even more concretely, shouldn't we be asking: What
route did changes in the social order and customary
practices in the Ch'ing dynasty follow? What sort of
social order was envisioned in the late Ming by these
low status, déclassé, young, and commoner elements if
it was not an expression of their customary practices?

In the late Ming-early Ch'ing period, Huang Tsung-
hsi was one example of a man who, while quintessentially
a literatus, not a lowly commoner, nevertheless dreamed
of a desirable future society. Mizoguchi Yūzō (in his
essay, "The Historical Place of the Ming-i tai-
fang-lu,"[b] (Hitotsubashi ronso 81.3) resolves the
problem of where Huang Tsung-hsi's political and
social thought differ from "populist" thought
advocated by a succession of thinkers since Mencius,
and the question of what sort of relationship such
thought bears with respect to Ch'ing rule. In one
sense, Huang's thought does discern an age after that
in which the social order has been turned upside down.
In contrast to earlier "populist" strains of thought
that posited a sovereign ministering to the state on
the basis of benevolence and kindness, according to
Mizoguchi, Huang's thought envisioned a political con-

stituency that took as its starting point the people
themselves seeking to realize their own private interests.
This contrast appears to be an elaboration of the comparison Mizoguchi made last year in his essay,[2] "The
Thought of the 'Tung-lin Faction,'"[a] between monarchy
based on the virtuous rule of the single monarch (i.e.,
benevolent despotism) and monarchy based on a division
of powers and public [i.e., joint] rule. This new
essay strengthens his case. One of his points, elaborated in this essay by reference to the Ming-i tai-fang
lu, is the connection between Huang's thought and the
Ch'ing regime. This connection could be foreseen in
his earlier essay where the political thought of the
Tung-lin clique, namely, division of powers and public
rule, are shown to have become reality because of the
Ch'ing regime.

However, the present argument is less persuasive
than the earlier one. First, it seems that the root of
this ideology of the division of power and public rule,
which, according to Mizoguchi, the Tung-lin clique and
Huang Tsung-hsi advocated, was to be underlain by local
public opinion. Huang Tsung-hsi's concept of a school
system, which has been evaluated as "serving the role
of an assembly in representative government" (Ojima
Sukema) and as "the incipient idea of representative
government of the old-democratic type" (Hou Wai-lu),
[can be viewed as an approach which] combined local
public opinion with disturbances directed against the
local officialdom (sheng-yüan riots). We might consider this perspective to be wrong and hold, as
Mizoguchi puts it, that Huang Tsung-hsi's views were
adopted by the Ch'ing regime. Witness for example the
fact that according to the Ch'ien-lung K'un-shan Hsin-
yang ho-chih, local public opinion as it was expressed
at the Confucian temple through the early years of the
K'ang-hsi reign played a major role in policy decisions

of the district magistrate. But then how do we explain
the fact that early in the Yung-cheng period, "because
the laws were strict, the gentry did not dare to open
their mouths on matters related to contemporary politics,
and the proceedings at the Confucian temple were all
form and no content"? Clearly such a towering current
could not be completely dammed up, and if the Tung-lin
clique's ideas had not been accommodated in some form or
other, the Ch'ing system itself could not have been
maintained. However, when local public opinion, which
should have provided a basis for the division of power
and public rule (or, in other words, which should have
acted as the starting point for self-interest), became
purely formalistic by virtue of the power of the Ch'ing
state, the "populist" views which Huang Tsung-hsi and
others advocated seem to have been driven into an
impasse. Surely this cannot be explained as essentially
due to the authority of the Ch'ing regime. Moreover,
when we think of the ferocious critiques of monarchy
expressed by such men as T'an Ssu-t'ung at the end of
the Ch'ing, doubts remain about the purported change
pointed out by Mizoguchi in the principal contradiction
under the Ch'ing regime.

    Shōji Sōichi's essay, "Unknown Anecdotes about
Kuei Yu-kuang: The Case of a Woman Named Chang"[a] (in
Kaga ronshū) is noteworthy as a fascinating description
of the power relations and human relations which comprised the social order in one locality. In 1544 a
young woman was murdered in Chia-ting prefecture,
Kiangsu. Taking the crime as indicative of a "change
in the times," Kuei Yu-kuang described the hostilities
as well as linkages among a wider variety of classes
and groups (the husband of the woman, her in-laws, and
her own parents, as well as the local magistrate, local
bosses, chü-jen, sheng-yüan, and the populace) that
lay behind the hushing up and resolution of the

incident. It offers us important material for a consideration of what sort of power went into making up
a local social order.

In his essay, "A Study of the Hsüan-chiang Dia-
grams in the Late Ming and Early Ch'ing"[a] (Tōkyō gakugei daigaku kiyō-Jimbun kagaku 30), Ōmura Kōdō discusses
the forms in which the six edicts of Ming T'ai-tsu and
the sixteen maxims of the K'ang-hai Emperor's imperial
edict were enunciated. Based on the hsüan-chiang forms
which are presented here, we can catch a glimpse of the
social order in one local setting (for example, the
relationship between local gentry and sheng-yüan).
According to Ōmura, the Ch'ing's rural compact (hsiang-
yüeh) was a religious ritual, certainly never based on
ethical, moral, or power relations or on political
authority. Thus, it transcended these [considerations]
and possessed a certain magical significance. The
characters, hsüan-chiang, Ōmura explains, mean "to sing"
and "to lecture" respectively. His argument becomes
extremely interesting when we consider the following
two points: (a) the magical powers of village headmen
and the singing as well as the lecturing aspects of
hsüan-chiang are stipulated in the sixteen maxims of
K'ang-hsi's imperial edict that appear on the title
page of the Pao-chüan, a collection of popular religious
canons; and (b) the chanting of scripture clearly
involved both singing and lecturing, and was called
hsüan-chüan. We hope to see many more essays like
Ōmura's in the future.

Sōda Hiroshi's essay, "The World of San-yen"[a]
(Fukuoka kyōiku daigaku kiyō 28), should be mentioned
as an attempt to uncover the consciousness or the
thought that underlay everyday life for the masses of
Chinese people. Until now the san-yen [three collections of Ming short stories--JAF] have been frequently
used by such scholars as Fu I-ling and Teng T'o to

supplement primary source materials in social and
economic history.   They have also been used to a
certain extent by such scholars as Ono Shihei, Saeki
Yūichi, and Tanaka Masatoshi, as sources through which
popular consciousness can be gleaned.   This essay is,
however, apparently the first attempt to confront
directly such issues as the meaning of <u>chin</u> (gold)
among the people, their view of the literati and ruling
class, their rationality, and their virtues of "integ-
rity" and "seriousness."   But there is still a problem
here.   In the biographies of merchants, which Sōda does
not make use of, we have evidence that they were never
separated from their books even while on the road
engaged in business activities and that these pseudo-
literati were often dignified as "noble" or "virtuous."

Shouldn't we thus try to understand the nature of
the relationship between the people's consciousness
and their social norms, on the one hand, and those of
the literati, on the other?   I also have serious reser-
vations about two other points: (a) Sōda claims that
the significance of "dignity" and "seriousness" gradually became increasingly emphasized among the people
from the Sung, through the Yüan, and into the Ming, but
mightn't this same trend have occurred even earlier,
although expressed in different words?   (b)   Are the <u>li</u>
in popular usage here and the <u>li</u> of Sung learning
entirely the same, as Sōda suggests?

What is beyond doubt, however, is that Sōda, taking
a different approach, achieves a higher level than does
Iwama Kazuo, who is similarly concerned with popular
thought.   After Iwama investigates the thought of Wang
Ken and Lo Ju-fang, he remarks: "The fact that no
results at all were produced is clear enough even
without Max Weber; a magical world view is clearly the
answer" ("'Popular' Thought in Feudal Chinese Society,"[b] <u>Hōsei ronshū</u> 77).

We should also note Shiba Yoshinobu's "A Ming
Merchant's Guidebook: An Analysis of the K'o-shang
i-lan hsing-mi t'ien-hsia"[a] (in Mori ronshū) which
seeks to elucidate business ethics. Shiba educes from
this text as virtues valued by merchants shame, frugal-
ity, humility, constancy, impartiality, sincerity, reli-
ability, maturity, and decisiveness; and he attempts to
connect the social import contained in commercial texts
with the social mobility between gentry and merchants.
The issue he raises has to do with the relationship
between the principles of competition that appear in
these commercial texts and the order in the society to
which these men belong. We would like to know how the
concept of a differentiation between internally and
externally oriented ethics, which the late Professor
Niida Noboru demonstrated for Chinese guilds, is to be
dealt with from now on, either positively or negatively.

I should like to discuss articles below according
to genre. The major works in the field of socio-economic history are as follows. Kanazawa Yō's essay,
"Kilns and Their Activities Among the People of Fukien
in the Ming Dynasty"[a] (Mindaishi kenkyū 7), finds, on
the basis of archeological reports and local gazetteers,
that nearly half of the departments and districts of
Fukien had local kilns, but that the ceramics they
produced did not match in either quality or quantity
ceramics from Ching-te-chen.

Three essays energetically analyze their respective sources to investigate themes relating to gentry
theory: Suzuki Hiroyuki, "An Analysis of Pao-lan in
the Late Ming"[a] (Shūkan Tōyōgaku 41); Nishimura
Kazuyo, "Nu-p'u in the Ming"[b] (Tōyōshi kenkyū 38.1);
and Miki Satoshi, "The Pao-chia System in Fukien in the
Late Ming"[a] (Tōyō gakuhō 61.1-2).

Nishimura discusses the background for the emergence of nu-p'u (bond-servants) as well as their duties.

She also looks into the process by which the regulations
covering nu-p'u status, which was clearly defined in
the early Ming, gradually became reduced to a shadow of
their former selves, as the distinction between "regular
commoner" and "demeaned" status crumbled. She considers
the primary cause of this change to lie in the military
strength through which the gentry sought to expand
their personal territorial control. Employed to this
end by the gentry, the nu-p'u gradually distanced themselves from direct gentry supervision; and, taking
advantage of the authority of the gentry, they continued to maximize their own personal advantage.

Miki concentrates on the issue of the relationship
between the gentry and the pao-chia system in the Wan-li
reign. He argues that the pao-chia system at that time
was an institution that sought to overcome the crisis
caused by the increasing numbers of peasant rebellions.
It was consistent with the movement of national authority toward assuming the role of direct intermediary
between landlord and tenants. Thus, the pao-chia
system sought to strengthen gentry control based on
an integration of national authority and the gentry.

Kawakatsu Mamoru, in his essay "The Social
Structure of the Early Modern Chinese City--Late Ming-
Early Ch'ing Cities in Kiangnan"[c] (Shichō N.S. 6),
studies the circumstances whereby the Department of
Duties and the Office of Sub-District Magistrate,
established from the late Ming in urban centers,
gradually cut back their scope and were dissolved.
He points out first that the administrative status of
cities was falling. Furthermore, he considers the
gradual urbanization of the gentry as well as the
actual situation of urban vagrants. Fuma Susumu has
added a critique to this essay in the form of a commentary.

Morita Akira's essay, "Water Utilization by the

Cities of Huai-an in the Ch'ing Period"[a] (Chūgoku suiri
shi kenkyū 9), is also a kind of urban study, based on
an analysis of the changes in the management of the
waterways and canals in and around the city of Huai-an.
According to Morita, canal management depended on
official funds in the hands of local officials by the
time of the late Ming. In the early Ch'ing, however,
although official cooperation and assistance were forth-
coming, an autonomous administrative structure centering
on the gentry class in the city was formed. Like Kawakatsu, Morita analyzes this structure in terms of a
"theory of the gentry." Perhaps the tax assessed on
dwelling construction[3] (chien-chia shui) was itself
included in what was generally referred to as official
funds, used for the purpose of employing men. To carry
this study further, one should reinvestigate the essential meaning of this tax which was linked to public
utilities.

Nakayama Mio's work, "Fluctuations in Commodity
Prices in the Kiangnan Region in the Early Ch'ing"[b]
(Tōyōshi kenkyū 37.4) continues her work of the previous year,[4] "Secular Trends in Rice Prices in Kiangnan
During the Early Ch'ing,"[a] and is a study of basic importance. She looks into the price changes in raw
cotton, raw silk thread, cotton cloth, and agricultural
land, all of which kept step for the most part with
rice prices. She points out that prices rose from the
late Ming into the early Shun-chih years, fell in the
K'ang-hsi era, and rose again sharply in the Ch'ien-
lung years. This kind of research is absolutely indis-
pensable for understanding the actualities of urban
life and the changing statuses of direct producers.
However, the scale of fluctuation for cotton textile
calendering in Soochow which she presents is incomplete.
Although there are numerous missing characters in the
inscription of Ch'ien-lung 4 (1739), just as in the

regulations of K'ang-hsi 59 (1722), there is no mistak-
ing the order that called for a sliding system of wages
at the time of the rise in rice prices, and the edict
of Ch'ien-lung 44 (1779) should be taken in the same
way. Thus, although we can assuredly point to a
decrease in real wages, there remains plenty of room
for additional research into whether or not we can
assert that, compared to the rate of increase in rice
prices, the rate of price increase for cotton textile
calendering was much lower.

Fujii Hiroshi's essay, "The Basic Structure of the
One Field-Two Owners System"[a] (two parts, Kindai
Chūgoku 5, 6), attempts to reanalyze fully the system
whereby one piece of land had two owners. This essay
remains unfinished as yet; the full argument, which
will encompass the Ming and Ch'ing, will be developed
in later numbers of Kindai Chūgoku.

A number of essays were published in the field of
Sino-Japanese and Sino-Ryūkyū diplomatic history:
Takase Kyōko, "The Posture Assumed by the Ryūkyū Kingdom Toward China in the Ming-Ch'ing Transition"[a]
(Ochanomizu shigaku 22); Kishaba Kazutaka, "Kamotsu-
roku: Inventory of Cargo Brought by Chinese on Pirate
Ships in K'ang-hsi 58 [1719]"[a] (Kaiji shi kenkyū 32);
and Matsuura Akira, "Shippers in China in the Nagasaki
Trade: Official and Popular Sino-Japanese Trade from
the Ch'ien-lung to the Hsien-feng Reigns"[a] (Shakai
keizai shigaku 45.1). Ms. Takase discusses the changing policy of the Ryūkyūs, which had become a tributary
state to China, during the period in which the Ch'ing
regime was establishing itself. Kishaba and Matsuura
are primarily concerned with the introduction and pre-
sentation of historical materials.

In the field of institutional history, we have the
following two essays: Matsumoto Takaharu, "The Political Aims of the Hung-wu Emperor's Reform of the

Educational System"[a] (Shikan 101); and Kawagoe Yasuhiro,
"On the Appointment to Provincial Military Posts of Wei-
so Officials in the Ming: The Wei-hsüan-fu"[a] (Chūō
daigaku bungakubu kiyō-Shigakka 24). Until now, Ming
T'ai-tsu's educational reforms have been studied as
educational and academic history. In contrast, Matsumoto argues, on the basis of an analysis of the school
regulations of 1382, that the objectives of the educational reforms were to bring under control the local
literati, landlords, and wealthy peasants right at the
prefectural, district, and departmental schools. Kawagoe introduces an historical source of basic importance,
the Wei-hsüan-fu (family registers of military officials
in the wei-so system), in order to clarify the Ming
military system. He also analyzes the career patterns
and qualifications of men appointed to provincial military posts. In recent years Kawagoe's work has helped
gradually to elucidate the Ming military system, previously not well understood.

A number of essays were published concerning the
history of popular and religious rebellions. Chūgoku
minshū hanran shi[2] (History of popular uprisings in
China) has selectively translated and annotated materials relating to rebellion from the Ming-shih chi-
shih pen-mo, the Ming-shih, the Shuang-huai sui-ch'ao,
and the Chien-chün li-lüeh. These selections are
included in the following sections of the book: "Popular Rebellions of the Late Yüan,"[b] translated, annotated, and introduced by Sakakura Atsuhide and Danjō
Hiroshi; and "Two Great Rebellions of the Mid-Ming,"[b]
translated, annotated, and introduced by Nishimura
Genshō.

Wada Masahiro's "A Peasant Rebellion in the Village
of Ch'ing-yang"[c] (Kyūshū daigaku Tōyōshi ronshū 7)
investigates a rebellion that occurred in 1801 in the
village of Ch'ing-yang, which was situated at the

juncture of the three provinces of Pei-chihli, Honan,
and Shansi. Wada questions whether the character yao
in the expression yao-t'ieh can be taken for the government's forced labor for the defense of the passes,
and argues that the expression referred to is yu-t'ieh
[a ledger for certifying payment of taxes--JAF]. He
argues that the immediate cause of the rebellion was
the resistance of the powerful and rich peasants to
the magistrate's labor conscription, but a doubt
lingers as to whether we can take this individual case
as the case for all participants in the rebellion.

Chikusa Masaaki's essay, "The Case of Prince Chu
San: An Investigation of a Secret Society in Kiangnan
in the Early Ch'ing"[a] (Shirin 62.4), criticizes previous studies which have regarded Chang Nien-i of Ta-
lan-shan in Chekiang as the same as I-nien ho-shang of
T'ai-ch'iang department in Kiangsu. He concludes that
the two men led bands that were entirely different in
nature.

Satō Kimihiko's essay, "An Analysis of the Rebellion of the Ch'ing-hui Sect of Wang Lun in 1774: An
Introduction to a Theory of the Boxers"[a] (Hitotsubashi
ronsō 81.3), tries to understand popular consciousness
in terms of the formation and travels of a rebellious
group. In this case, government troops, attempting to
negate the spells and magic of the "spirit women"
(shen-nü) who were attacking their city, fought back
by using polluting substances. Satō interprets this as
the opposition of the "profane" (official forces)
versus the "sacred" (the rebels). In this way he
offers us a rather unique perspective in this article.

Studies of Ch'ing intellectual history, and particularly of k'ao-cheng-hsüeh in the Ch'ien-lung and
Chia-ch'ing years, have been steadily accumulating in
recent years. Hamaguchi Fujio's essay, "The Background
to the Establishment of Ch'ing Scholarship"[a] (Tōhōgaku

58), traces the intellectual links between hsin-hsüeh in
the Ming and textual criticism in the Ch'ing on the basis
of the interrelatedness of the thought of Wang Yang-ming,
Li Chih, Ku Yen-wu, and Huang Tsung-hsi. Similar studies
have been done in the United States. One such piece is
Edward Ch'ien, "Chiao Hung and the Revolt against Ch'eng-
Chu Orthodoxy," in The Unfolding of Neo-Confucianism
(ed. Wm. T. deBary, Columbia University Press, 1975).

Eguchi Hisao's "Studies in the History of the Flow
of Silver by Statecraft Thinkers of the Ch'ing: The Early
19th Century"[a] (Shakai keizai shigaku 45.2) analyzes how
studies of the flow of silver, begun by Ku Yen-wu, were
continued and developed by Ting Lü-heng, Miu Tzu, Huang
Ju-ch'eng, and Sun Ting-ch'en. This piece is especially
important for its comprehensive view of Ch'ing scholarly
studies in economic history, but unfortunately Ku Yen-wu's
fundamental research has been partially ignored. If
Eguchi tries to understand Sun Ting-ch'en through a comparison with Ku Yen-wu, then he should at least confront
Ku's "I-ch'ien wei-fu" in chuan 11 of the Jih-chih lu and
Ku's "Ch'ien-liang lun" in chuan 1 of T'ing-lin wen-chi.
And he should study these in comparison with Sun's arguments. Ichiko Shōzō has also written on the study of
currency in the Ch'ing: "An Analysis of the History of
Currency in the Ch'ing: The Phenomenon of Prizing Silver
and Denigrating Copper and Its Origins in the Chia-ch'ing
and Tao-kuang Reigns"[a] (Takushoku daigaku ronshū 121).

In his fascinating essay, "An Approach to Ch'ing
Scholarship: Chu Yün, Shao Chin-han, Hung Liang-chi,
and Chang Hsüeh-ch'eng"[a] (Tōhōgaku 57), Kawata Teiichi
discusses the various associations among that group of
scholars who gathered around the great patron Chu Yün
in the Ch'ien-lung and Chia-ch'ing eras. Also, as has
been the case in recent studies of Ch'ing intellectual
history, Kawata frequently deals with what lies behind
the methodology of the k'ao-cheng scholars. But, by
this he most assuredly does not mean "substructure"

[i.e., economic developments--JAF].

In his essay, "The Scholarship of Wang Nien-sun"[a] (in Kaga ronshū), Kondō Mitsuo argues that Wang's k'ao-cheng research did not develop from an inductive method based on comparative textual documentation, but was founded on the idea of hsing-ling (to know the meaning in one's mind).

Yamaguchi Hisakazu's essay, "From Existence to Ethics: The Philosophy of Wang Fu-chih's Shang-shu yin-i"[a] (Tōhōgaku 57), investigates Wang Fu-chih's thought as revealed in the Shang-shu yin-i. He argues that although Wang recognized the interdependence between heaven and man, he distinguished nature from human affairs and laws from ideals. While affirming the position occupied by men in the universe, he tried to extend this relationship to an ethical philosophy.

In his essay, "Tai Chen's Phonology: His Concerns and His Scholarship"[b] (Tōhōgaku 58), Kinoshita Tetsuya liberates Tai Chen's phonological research from the framework of "studies of ancient pronunciation" which had already begun by that time. Kinoshita takes a fresh look at Tai Chen's phonology on the basis of his epistemology. He points out that by doing research into the ancient pronunciation of characters Tai Chen was merely trying to present a corroborative source for seeking "restraint" that he considered innate to mankind.

Kinoshita uses a similar analytic method in his essay, "Tuan Yü-ts'ai's Modes of Thought"[b] (Chūgoku shisō shi kenkyū 3), to point out that we can appreciate Tuan's mode of thought as having penetrated the realm of material things.

Honda Wataru's "On Reading the Tiao-ku-chi"[a] (in Mori ronshū) provides an explanation of Chiao Hsün's (1763-1820) Tiao-ku-chi. Honda also presents a study of Chiao's thought.

The field of Ming intellectual history has not in
recent years produced as much research as the Ch'ing
field. We have two studies. Yamashita Ryūji   "On
the Li-shih ts'ang-shu (Part 1)"[a] (in Mori ronshū)
presents an explanation of various sections of Li Chih's
Ts'ang-shu. Shibata Atsushi's "Feng Shao-hsü: The
Life and Thought of a Late Ming Literatus"[a] (Tetsugaku
nempō 38) analyzes Feng's thought from two perspectives:
the affirmation of the theory of innate goodness and
the observance of ritual. Shibata shows how the Kan-
hsiang school [i.e., the school of Chan Jo-shui--JAF]
was destined to bring a cooling off to the superheating
of the "mind" that the school of Wang Yang-ming has
stirred up.

Because of limited space, I will be unable to touch
on studies of literature and the arts. In the field of
bibliography, we have Katō Naoto's "A Study of Ch'ing
Imperial Diaries"[a] (Tōhōgaku 57), which presents materials relating to the imperial diaries of the Ch'ing
period. Also, Noguchi Tetsurō has completed his "Draft
of an Index to the Criminal Code in the Ming History"[a]
(Rekishi jinrui 5, 6, 7), which offers us research
tools of fundamental importance.

Several new books are also worthy of mention:
Mano Senryū, Mindai bunka shi kenkyū (Studies in Ming
Cultural History); Gotō Motomi, Min-Shin shisō to
Kirisuto kyō (Thought in the Ming-Ch'ing Period and
Christianity);[a] Araki Kengo, Minmatsu shūkyō shisō
kenkyū: Kan Tōmei no shōgai to shisō (A Study of Late
Ming Religious Thought: The Life and Thought of Kuan
Tung-ming);[a] Okada Hidehiro, Kōki tei no tegami (The
Letters of the K'ang-hsi Emperor);[a] and Igarashi
Masakazu, Chūgoku kinsei kyōiku shi no kenkyū (A Study
of Early Modern Chinese Educational History).[a] Mano's
book will soon be reviewed in Tōyōshi kenkyū. We hope
the others will be reviewed as well.

JAPANESE STUDIES OF POST-OPIUM WAR CHINA: 1979
Hamashita Takeshi, in
Shigaku zasshi 89.5
(May 1980), 212-19.

Investigations of the "international crisis" in
studies of modern Chinese history have shared a certain
common ground with diplomatic history or the history of
international relations when taken up as subjects for
research. However, the "international crisis" in Chinese history has frequently been considered as a point
of departure, in so far as we refer to it as the "foreign pressure" (or the "foreign cause"). And this in
turn has led to a deepening of research on domestic
Chinese history itself. To the extent that this "international crisis" is concerned with deriving the causes
of the development of Chinese history, it differs from
diplomatic history or the history of foreign relations.
Thus, when we investigate the "international crisis" in
Chinese history, particularly in modern history, we are
considering the historical significance of the internal
development of the subject under consideration. At the
same time, there is also a need for a clear methodological perspective to realize this end.

When analyzing the "international crisis," we can
use modern Chinese economic history as a research
model. This field had produced important research on
problems involving the analyses of individual commodities as well as analyses of capital investment. Each
of these commodities follows a pattern from foreign
trade [i.e., introduction into China--JAF] to domestic
production. For example, in the study of the cotton
industry, it has been argued that an investigation of

cotton thread and raw cotton will show the influence
exerted by trade relations on domestic cotton cloth
production, and that with the passing of time cotton
cloth production was linked to the problem of foreigners'
rights in the industries in which they invested capital
after the Sino-Japanese War (see below).

Structuring our framework for the studies of 1979
around this perspective, our analysis of individual
commodities follows in this order: opium, silk thread,
soybeans, tobacco.

In her article, "Opium Production in Szechwan at
the End of the Ch'ing"[a] (Tōyō gakuhō 60.3-4), Shinmura
Yōko first points out that the process by which Chinese-
produced opium gradually supplanted imported opium is
made clear by British consular and customs reports.
Next, she indicates that although high productivity in
Szechwan was based on advantageous conditions for agriculture there, the farmers had to rely on opium production for ready cash because of the chronic shortage
of currency. Cash was also needed because of the actual
requirements of poppy planting and the stringency of
landlord expropriations in cash from tenant farmers
(there were three types of tenant farmers: those who
either leased paddy land, hilly land, or land at river
dikes). As a result, this process brought about a
vicious cycle of insufficiency of grains and speculation,
and tenant farmers who relied on loaned provisions from
landlords and usurers were forced to stay in opium production. In conclusion, Shinmura argues that, contrary
to the views of Kubota Bunji, the possibility for large
tenant households to establish themselves in Szechwan
arose in the period of the 1860's and 1870's before the
appearance of land rent for lands relegated to opium
production. She also points out that large tenant
households, which pop up extensively at the height of
this period, had rather the character of usury

capitalists and were in fact landlords who lived off the
direct-producer peasants beneath them .

Next we have Kikuchi Kazutaka's essay, "Warlord
Control and Opium in Shensi: Peasant Rebellions of the
1920's and Early 1930's"[a] (Kindai Chūgoku 4). Kikuchi
clarifies the process by which landlords rescinded the
prohibition on tobacco and forced the cultivation of
poppies because from the late Ch'ing through the 1911
period cash crops under cultivation had shifted from
opium to raw cotton. The warlords then imposed a variety of taxes on the opium as a source of revenue.
While the warlords retained control of the transport
and exchange of the opium, the landlords simultaneously
extracted heavy rents to support the warlords and acted
as usurers. Peasant rebellions arose in opposition to
these rents and to the warlords. With this might
mustered behind them, peasant cooperative associations
were organized and had links with the soviets in North
Shensi and the Shensi-Kansu region as well as with the
Shen-Kan-Ning Soviet.

Mori Hisao, in his "The Problems of Controlling
Opium in Taiwan (Part 1)"[a] (Ajia keizai 19.11), begins
an analysis of how Japan's opium policy changed from
one of strict prohibition after the annexation of Taiwan
to one of toleration in conjunction with Taiwan's
becoming fiscally independent.

With respect to silk thread, Tajiri Toshi's essay,
"An Investigation Into the Policies to Promote Sericulture in Kiangsu in the Latter Half of the 19th
Century"[a] (Kagoshima keidai ronshū 19.4, 20.1),
analyzes policies for the encouragement of sericulture
that were advanced in the 1860's and 1870's primarily
by prefects and district magistrates who were trying to
promote recovery from the decline in agricultural productivity following the Taiping Rebellion and from
inactivity in the textile industry after the opening of

the treaty ports. Once Sericulture Bureaus (ts'an-sang
chü) and Bureaus of Public Sericulture (kung-sang chü)
were created, local gentry became the essential suppliers
of capital as well; they bought and raised mulberry seed-
lings from Hu-chou and distributed them gratis among the
people. Furthermore, they sent for men skilled at sericulture and had them teach the peasants techniques for
raising, cultivating, and producing silk. Tajiri feels
that he cannot give an unconditional evaluation of the
effectiveness of these policies, but he exhaustively
analyzes the historical materials bearing on the sericulture bureaus of Tan-t'u [Kiangsu], Ch'ing-ho [Shan-
tung], and Shanghai. He stresses the role played by
the local gentry in these cases.

In his article, "The Mechanical Silk-Reeling Industry in Kiangsu and Chekiang on the Eve of the Depression"[a] (Shirin 62.2), Okumura Satoshi criticizes previous
studies for applying to the entire mechanical silk-
reeling industry in Kiangsu and Chekiang the characteristics of Shanghai silk factories. He points out the
modern and distinctly Chinese nature of "local silk-
reeling factors" which were newly established in the
cocoon breeding centers of Chekiang and Wu-hsi.

Also, Sugiyama Nobuya has written on the trade in
raw silk thread: "A Quantitative Reevaluation of Raw
Silk Thread Exports in the Late Tokugawa and Early
Meiji Eras: Trends and Foreign Merchants on the London
and Lyons Markets"[a] (Shakai keizai shigaku 45.3). In
it he investigates the competition among Japanese,
Italian, Chinese, and Indian-made silk on the European
markets, using documents such as those from the British
Foreign Office and Jardine-Matheson.

Gonjō Yasuo, in his essay "The Overseas Activities
of Parisian Discount Banks in the Latter Half of the
19th Century: French Overseas Banks and East Asian
Markets"[a] (2 parts, Kinyū keizai 175, 176), makes use

of original documents to clarify the history of the
Parisian discount banks (in East Asian markets) that
were involved in the commercial circulation of raw silk
thread and in capital investment dealings. Gonjō's
article also aims at "shedding light on French capitalism in its decisive 19th century transition from 'lib-
eralism' to 'imperialism' by looking at the 'marginal
sector' of economic relations with respect to East
Asia." Thus, he raises the problem of the correct
methodological approach for clarifying the international
opportunities for French capitalism.

In his essay, "A Reorganization of English Colonial
Banks: China and Japan, 1870-1890"[a] (2 parts, Keizaigaku ronshū 45.1, 45.3), Ishii Kanji describes the
peculiarities of Asia as an arena for the circulation
of silver coinage through an analysis of the history of
English colonial banks in Asia and the commercial activities of Jardine-Matheson and Company. The declining
value of silver from the 1870's on brought about a
reorganization of colonial banks. The reorganization
in turn led to the emergence of a sharp distinction
(being made on the part of the English bankers) between
China and Japan, with Japan becoming primary, particularly as Yokohama specie made inroads into China. Over
time the disparity between China and Japan grew even
larger.

Katō Yūzō's "Triangular Trade in Asia in the 19th
Century"[a] (Yokohama shiritsu daigaku ronsō Jimbun
kagaku keiretsu 30.2-3) takes great pains in attempting
to reckon trade volumes and quotas for various commercial goods, such as black tea, opium, and cotton
goods (including raw cotton and cotton thread) which
made up the triangular trade among England, India, and
China. Katō also discusses how one goes about making
such calculations.

On soybean meal fertilizer, we have Adachi Keiji's

article, "The Circulation of Soybean Meal Fertilizer
and Commercial Agriculture in the Ch'ing"[b] (Tōyōshi
kenkyū 37.3). Adachi first shows how the circulation
of soybean meal fertilizer, which reached its high
point in the mid-Ch'ing, depended on the development of
upper peasant (shang-nung) and rich peasant (fu-nung)
land management. Secondly, because of the importation
of Western goods and the creation of the likin around
the time of the opening of the treaty ports, there was
a rise in the cost of soybean meal fertilizer, a decline
in the cost of manufactured goods, and a rise in wages.
He points out as well the overall retrogression of commercial fertilizer circulation and the retrogression in
commercial agriculture in the lower Yangtze delta
which resulted. Thus, the problem raised here is the
same as that of the relationship between Western and
native textiles: the circulation of goods which supported the growth of domestic markets was cut off
because of links with foreign markets, and small commodity production in the lower Yangtze, which had
reached a high level, reverted from hired labor back
to family labor.

In his essay, "A Study of Tobacco Cultivation in
Modern China: Shantung in the Early 20th Century"[a]
(Shakai keizai shigaku 45.1), Uchiyama Masao analyzes
how, under the objective conditions of strengthening
cohesion of the international market that accompanied
the opening of the railways, American-style tobacco was
introduced as a commercial crop that could be sold off
at a high price to Euro-American industrial capitalists.
Uchiyama differs in emphasis with the argument of
Yoshida Kōichi, and says that peasants, who were
engaged in the cultivation of cash crops even though
they had to purchase necessary foodstuffs, sought, while
their relative impoverishment proceeded, a "secure"
agricultural management system for the maintenance of

small-scale enterprises without severing "impoverished
enterprises or starved commercial agriculture." This
situation had existed earlier when Euro-American industrial capital dominated the rural village through
the intermediary of commercial and usury capital.

Finally, let me address the articles which deal
with the cotton industry. Ishii Mayako's essay, "The
Movement of English Capital in the Latter Half of the
19th Century: The Case of Jardine-Matheson and Company"[a] (Shakai keizai shigaku 45.4), elucidates
business conditions in quantitative terms on the basis
of original Company documents. She also analyzes the
diversification of management and the growth of capital
exports from the 1870's. In particular, she stresses
that capital made inroads into China through ties with
the Hong Kong-Shanghai Bank. She feels we should pay
close attention to the activities of Foreign Office
bureaucrats stationed in China, such as the English
consul in Shanghai, in dealing with the issue of the
manufacturing rights granted to foreigners after the
Sino-Japanese War. Several of the points that have
hitherto fallen within the realm of conjecture are here
substantiated by source materials. Furthermore, this
essay is worthy of evaluation from the perspective of
foreign concerns, such as with respect to the actual
content of "partnerships."

Kuwabara Tetsuya's essay, "Plans for Direct
Capital Investment by the Japanese Spinning Industry
[in China] just after the Sino-Japanese War: The Case
of the Tung-hua Spinning Company"[a] (Keizai keiei ronsō
14.2), traces the plans for expansion of the Tung-hua
Spinning Company through acquisition of manufacturing
rights. He follows their activities through to the
withdrawal of the plan because of taxes imposed by the
Chinese government on industrial goods, and eventually
to the company's collapse. His descriptions of the

arguments put forward by the Japanese spinning industry
for constructive action and their machinations arising
out of fear of competition with Europe and America are
fascinating.

As we have seen above, an analysis that traces the
history of individual commodities extends to problems of
the function of those commodities in international markets, their domestic circulation, and their production
in rural villages; and each history is punctuated by
the Opium War, the Sino-Japanese War, and the 1911
Revolution. I do not believe we have yet reached a
thesis which synthesizes all these aspects, but two
themes must be addressed when we analyze past research:
(a) how can we coordinate the interrelationships of the
various issues raised in individual analyses; and (b)
how can we transcend the contradictions between the
limitations of local regions and the extension (or
diffusion) of the argument to various related spheres?
For an overview of recent research, there is: Tanaka
Masatoshi, "China: Economic History,"[a] in Hatten tojō
kokukenkyū: Nanajūnendai Nihon ni okeru seika to kadai
(Japanese Research on the Road to Development: Results
and Themes in the 1970's).

Next, let us look at studies of the problem of
capital investment. Sasaki Yō's essay, "The International Politics Surrounding the Russo-French Loan to
China in 1895"[a] (Shigaku zasshi 88.7), addresses the
formation of the Russo-French loan not simply as a
fiscal problem, but as an expression also of a political issue of major diplomatic importance to the
Powers and to China. From this perspective, Sasaki
argues that for the Ch'ing dynasty the issue of the
loan changed in essence from a local fiscal problem to
a national fiscal one to a national political issue.
Sasaki has also written a piece entitled "Studies in
the Modern History of Sino-Russian Relations: The Era

of the Sino-Japanese War"[b] (Kindai Chūgoku 5).

 Watanabe Atsushi's article, "The Reform Movement
in the Salt Administration at the Time of the 1911
Revolution (Part II): The Controversy between the
Reformers and the Conservatives"[a] (Kumamoto daigaku
kyōiku gakubu kiyō 28), argues that the key to Yüan
Shih-k'ai's establishment of political power lay in
financial administration and that he took full advantage of this possibility through fiscal assistance
(relief loans) from the imperialist powers. The salt
tax became the primary security for the loans, although
it was not necessarily a stable source of revenue: on
the one hand, there were demands from foreign banking
interests for [powers of] supervision and control over
Chinese finances, and, on the other, there was at this
juncture a movement on the Chinese side for the reform
of the salt administration. After analyzing the course
taken by the negotiations over the loans, Watanabe
traces the development from (a) opposition in the
assemblies between the reformist group's Chang Chien,
Director of the Salt Administration, and the conser-
vative party's Chou Hsüeh-hsi, head of fiscal administration, to (b) the shelving of the whole issue.
Throughout this entire process Watanabe points out as
well the resistance of salt merchants to reform. We
anticipate further work from him on this last point.

 In his article, "Capital Investment in Chinese
Railroads in the Early 20th Century: On the Railroad
Rights Recovery Movement"[a] (Ajia keizai 20.5), Sōda
Saburō points out that when studying the railroad
rights recovery movement we must analyze not only what
sort of force developed into what kind of opposition
movement to the Ch'ing government's railway policy, but
we must also look at the problem of local railroad
capital accumulation by the railroad companies and the
provincial assemblies. These assemblies were estab-

lished by the Ch'ing as a representative form of government in preparation for adoption of a constitutional
system. Sōda investigates methods of capital procurement by the railroad companies and the provincial
assembly in Hunan (known as shang-ku, tsu-ku, and fang-
ku).[1] These methods became the impetus for a strong
reaction to the introduction of loans for the railway
lines. He concludes that these capital procurement
methods in fact more closely resembled a form of
taxation.

Ajioka Tōru's essay, "The Chinese Nationalist
Movement in the Early Years of World War I: The Twenty-
One Demands and the Chinese People"[a] (Rekishigaku kenkyū,
special issue), is concerned with the development of
the national revolutionary movement from the 1911 Revolution to the May Fourth Movement. He discusses the
boycott of Japanese goods and the movement for saving
the nation and saving money led by Yüan Shih-k'ai, who
ingratiated himself with the boycott efforts. Later,
Yüan's movement developed into a capital accumulation
effort by the bourgeoisie.

In his essay, "A Study of the New Four Nation
Loan Consortium: The Opposition between the Powers and
the Chinese National Movement up to the Washington
Conference"[a] (Nihon shi kenkyū 203), Akashi Iwao
studies this loan consortium, founded in 1920, and sees
the cause of its failure in China's internal political
and economic relationships and in the people's opposition movement. Along these same lines is the essay by
Sugano Tadashi, "The Twenty-One Demands and the Anti-
Japanese Boycott by Overseas Chinese"[a] (Tōkai daigaku
bungakubu kiyō 31).

Two articles that point out how the loans became
serious domestic issues causing opposition even in the
countries that offered them are: Matsuda Takeshi,
"The Wilson Government and Wall Street: The Withdrawal

of the Six Nation Loan Consortium"[a] (Seiyō shigaku 112,
113); and Ikegami Kazuo, "The Loans to China: The Overseas Business Activities of the Deposit Bureau of the
Finance Ministry"[a] (Hitotsubashi ronsō 71.6).

Analyses of capital investment thus advance us one
step further from the level of investigating the process
by which loans given led to the acquisition of rights:
they also provide us with a way to understand simultaneously in what way and in which spheres in China this
invested capital functioned and the concrete activities
by which capital was procured at the local level.
Studies addressing these issues have been accumulating
in recent years.

Let us consider essays concerning the "international
crisis" outside the field of economic history. In his
as yet unfinished article, "A Study of the Opium War:
From the British Army's Invasion of Canton to the Dismissal of [Sir Charles] Elliot as Plenipotentiary"[a]
(Kindai Chūgoku, 5, 6), Sasaki Masaya elucidates in
great detail the period from the rupture (beginning
January 1841) of the Ch'uan-pi Treaty between British
Plenipotentiary Elliot and Ch'ing Imperial Commissioner
Ch'i-shan through the invasion of Canton and its ces-
sation.

In his essay, "Lin Tse-hsü's Policy of Resistance
to the English and His Thought"[a] (Tōyōshi kenkyū 38.3),
Tanaka Masayoshi presents the argument that Lin's
intellectual progression, manifested in his new knowledge of the West, became a "Chinese knowledge" transcending the framework of past sinocentric thought.
This [new mentality] provided the intellectual basis
both for his strengthening of Kwangtung's defenses and
for his opposition to the British. With his ability
to judge the people's strengths, Lin was able to con-
centrate all these efforts against the British.

Hayashi Tatsurō's article, "The Taipings and the

Powers, 1853-54"[a] (Tōyō gakuhō 60.3-4), discusses the
four meetings between various national delegations and
the Taipings. He argues that the Powers, who claimed
neutrality, clearly opposed the Taipings. The Western
nations took part in the war in order to extract advan-
tages from the Chinese and never assumed a neutrality
of the sort that called for equal national relations
with both the Ch'ing and the Taiping rebels.

We also have Miura Tetsuaki's essay, "An Analysis
of the Sino-Japanese Treaty on Friendship and Commerce:
The Starting Point in Modern History of Unamicable
Sino-Japanese Relations"[a] (Kaigai jijō 27.1). Miura
argues that Japan, having planned to invade China in
imitation of the West, witnessed a heightening of the
call to invade Korea and Taiwan in the same year, sent
troops to Taiwan the next year, and forced a treaty on
her which was "equal" in name but not in reality. He
also has written "America's Demand for Most-Favored
Nation Status in China"[b] (Kaigai jijō 27.3).

Abe Seiji's essay, "Russia's Far Eastern Policy and
the Occupation of Kushunkotan on Sakhalin"[a] (Shakai
keizai shigaku 45.4), discusses the Russian occupation
of Kushunkotan from the autumn of 1853 till the spring
of 1854 as an example of the change in Russian policy
in the Far East. Abe differs from the conventional
wisdom in pointing out two active factions in Russian
domestic politics before the Crimean War of the mid-
19th century: (1) hardliners in government, officials
on the scene in the Far East, and Nicolas I who pre-
ferred military actions to expand Russian territories
in the East; and (2) the main faction within the government who wanted a policy of friendship with China and
with Japan, which would create the basis from which to
develop markets for industrial goods and for future
overseas trade.

Kani Hiroaki, in his essay "On the Mutiny of Chi-

nese Coolies on Board the Peruvian Ship Cayalti"[a]
(Shigaku 49.2-3), analyzes a mutiny on board the
Cayalti along the Peruvian coast in 1868 and the entry
of the ship later into the port of Hakodate en route
home. He understands the coolie trade to have developed from a situation in which Euro-American capital,
faced with a severe shortage of labor because of the
emancipation of the black slaves, was seeking in Ch'ing
China, newly defeated in the Opium War, a replacement
supply of labor. Kani's book-length study, Kindai
Chūgoku no kūri to "choka" (Coolies in China and "Chu-
hua"),[b] has recently been published. It enables us now
to come to terms with the worldwide movement of Chinese
laborers, but it deserves a longer, separate review.

Banno Masataka has written "Ma Chien-chung's
Mission to India in 1881: His Travel Account, Nan
Hsing Chi"[a] (Shakai kagaku jānaru 17).[3] Ma Chien-chung,
as unofficial envoy for Li Hung-chang in 1881, was able
to gain insight into the plans of governmental officials
in India for the gradual decrease in opium traffic.
Banno provides an introduction and explication of Ma's
fascinating account of his trip from Tientsin to Simura
to investigate the opium situation.

Kataoka Kazutada's article, "The Muslim Rebellion
in Kansu, 1895-96"[a] (Ōsaka kyōiku daigaku kiyō 27.2-3),
analyzes local differences within the great uprising in
Kansu that spread to twenty-three counties. He considers the underlying cause to have been ethnic antipathy between Muslim and Han. We anticipate further
pieces on the political and economic content of this
ethnic antipathy which was related to the Ch'ing government's basic policy of keeping Han and Muslim separate.

In his essay, "The Siberian War and the May Fourth
Movement,"[a] (Rekishigaku kenkyū, special issue), Nozawa
Yutaka examines the Siberian War as an expression of

the issue of revolution-counterrevolution involving all
of East Asia. He claims that we must reconsider the
May Fourth Movement from this perspective.

Mori Tokihiko's article, "A Short History of the
Work-Study Movement in France"[a] (Tōhō gakuhō 50, 51),
makes use of materials from a volume he translated
(together with Kawata Teiichi): Ho Ch'ang-kung, Ch'in-
kung chien-hsüeh sheng-huo hui-i (Memoirs of Life in
the Work-Study Movement).[a] Making liberal use of this
source, he reconstructs the actual history of the work-
study movement and demonstrates that it was an out-
growth of the May Fourth Movement. This essay itself
deserves a longer review.

The essay, "The Institute for the Natural Sciences
in Shanghai: A Study of Cultural Enterprises with
Respect to China"[b] (Tōkyō joshi daigaku ronshū 30.1) by
Yamane Yukio, and Abe Hiroshi's essay, "Japanese
'Cultural Enterprises in China' and Chinese Educational
and Cultural Circles in the Late 1920's"[a] (Kan 8.5-6),
both present analyses of activities known as "cultural
enterprises." In addition, both point out forcefully
that under the political circumstances of the time it
was impossible for cultural enterprises to function
purely as such.

Research on Manchuria and Taiwan in Japanese
historical studies has developed as a problem of markets in the history of Japanese capitalist expansion
and overseas colonial rule. However, there remains
the issue of how we are to understand this expansion
from the Chinese side. The essays contained in the
two volumes--Nihon teikoku shugi to higashi Ajia (Japanese Imperialism and East Asia) and Taiwan kin-gendaishi
kenkyū (Studies in the Modern and Contemporary History
of Taiwan, vol. 2)--raise many issues for discussion,
but I should like to leave their elucidation for later
book reviews.

We have a number of discussions of the village:
Nakagane Katsuji, "Village Structure in [the region that
was formerly] Manchuria: A Preliminary Study"[a] (Ajia
kenkyū 25.3-4); Ishida Hiroshi, "The Social Structure of
Chinese Villages in Taiwan: A Field Study of Ten Villages in Tai-nan County, Tso-chen hsiang"[a] (Ajia kenkyū
26.3); and Ishida Hiroshi, Eguchi Nobukiyo, and Kubota
Hiromu, "Village Temples in Taiwan: Villager Cohesion
as Seen Through the Temples"[a] (Kikan jinruigaku 10.1).
Essays concerning the anti-Japanese nationalist movement include: Itō Teruo, "Chiang Wei-shui and the Anti-
Japanese Nationalist Movement in Taiwan: Through the
Collapse of the Taiwan Cultural Association"[a] (Yokohama
shiritsu daigaku ronsō-Jimbun kagaku keiretsu 30.2-3);
and Wakabayashi Masahiro, "The Meaning of Tai-chi [waiting
for the right moment] for Huang Ch'eng-t'ing: The Anti-
Japanese Nationalist Thought of a Taiwanese Intellectual
Under Japanese Rule"[a] (in Taiwan kin-gendaishi kenkyū).

Let us conclude our discussion of works written from
the perspective of the "international crisis" and move on
to look at essays concerning other modern historical fields
as well as intellectual history. Kawabata Genji's "Several
Questions Raised by Li Hsiu-ch'eng's Personal Deposition"[a]
(Kindai Chūgoku 6) compares Li's handwritten deposition
with other historical evidence. Doi Hiromu's "Ch'en Yü-
ch'eng"[a] (Shien, Rikkyō daigaku shigakkai 39.2) is a short
biographical sketch of Ch'en. In "On Tung Hsün and His
Writings, Particularly His Diary"[a] (Kindai Chūgoku 4, 5),
Enoki Kazuo offers an introduction and explanation of
Tung's diary. His real-life descriptions in the diary do
not appear in his memorials, and thus make this work
particularly valuable. We anticipate more from Enoki
along this line.

Natsui Haruki's essay, "Gentry and Commoner Households and the Policies of Equalizing and Reducing the
Land Tax"[a] (Chūgoku kindaishi kenkyūkai tsūshin 8, 11),

analyzes the policies employed for lowering taxes and
prices in various central and southeastern provinces
mainly during the T'ung-chih reign. He also analyzes
the policy of "tax equalization" which was carried out
at the same time and the problem of correcting the disparity in the tax rates on "large" [i.e., gentry] versus
"small" [i.e., commoner] households--a problem which
became the object of reform at the time. Natsui concludes that, as a result of its complete dependence on
the gentry to solve its systemic crisis, the Ch'ing
underwent a metamorphosis from being a landlord-state
which, under the doctrine of an equal tax rate, looked
upon all landowners equally, to being a gentry-state
which conferred on the gentry official authority for
local control, with the gentry as its protective backbone.

We also have several studies of Liang Ch'i-ch'ao;
Kusunose Masaaki, "The Concept of Constitutionalism in
the Late Ch'ing: The Case of Liang Ch'i-ch'ao"[a]
(Shigaku kenkyū 143); Nagai Kazumi, "The Monarchial
Restoration Movement of 1917 and Liang Ch'i-ch'ao"[a]
(Jimbun kagaku ronshū 13, with further installments
expected); and Kawakami Tetsumasa, "Liang Ch'i-ch'ao
and the Anti-Yüan [Shih-k'ai] Movement"[a] (Gakushūin
shigaku 15). These articles are concerned, respectively, with Liang's constitutional thought, his views
on founding a constitutional system, and the movement
to restore the imperial institution. They analyze
Liang's development from pro-Yüan to anti-Yüan
positions.

Ono Shinji discusses the career of Yün Tai-ying
in his essay, "Idealism in the May Fourth Era: The
Case of Yün Tai-ying"[a] (Tōyōshi kenkyū 38.2). Ono
describes the process by which idealism pervaded Yün's
thinking and the difficulties he ran into with real-
life encounters along the way.

Kubota Bunji's article, "Yüan Shih-k'ai's Imperial Plans and the Twenty-One Demands"[a] (Shisō*20), investigates the historical sources in an attempt to elucidate in concrete terms the internal connections between Yüan's plans to make himself emperor and the Twenty-One Demands.

In his essay, "The Distribution of Same-Surname Villages in Lung-yu county, Chekiang"[a] (in Mori ronshū), Nakamura Tetsuo presents a water system theory in his quantitative analysis of same-surname villages. His analysis is consistent with the marketing-area theory of G. W. Skinner. Nakamura has also, in conjunction with Imai Seiichi and Harada Yoshio, translated Skinner's Marketing and Social Structure in Rural China [originally published by the Journal of Asian Studies in 1964 and 1965--JAF]. They review the history of research in this field in a detailed account at the end of the volume.

In their conflict with traditional consciousness during the fluid times of the late Ch'ing, Chinese intellectuals were attempting to clarify the temporal significance of their own historical position and their reform movement. In the realm of thought, they sought to come to terms with the tension between themselves and the times. We cannot examine all the problems of thought, but let us consider the following three essays: Nakashita Masaharu, "The Late Yen Fu"[a] (Tōyōgaku ronsō-Tōyō daigaku bungakubu kiyō 32, Bukkyō gakka, Chūgoku tetsugaku bungakka hen 4); Gotō Nobuko, "The Philosophy of Ts'ai Yüan-p'ei"[a] (Jimbun kagaku ronshū 13) and Kobayashi Takeshi, "Reading Chang Ping-lin: His Words and His World"[a] (in Mori ronshū).

Nakashita's viewpoint is that Yen Fu's thought in his last years was in a period of reidentification with tradition. From this perspective, he analyzes the changes in Yen's evaluation of Yüan Shih-k'ai, his

patriotism, and the transformation in his views on the
polity from republicanism to constitutional monarchism.
Gotō discusses Ts'ai Yüan-p'ei's world view and his
philosophy of life. From them Ts'ai drew a view of man
based on nationality which possessed the behavioral
principle of "for the group" (ch'ün). Gotō argues that
Ts'ai tried to submerge the divergence between his ideal
and reality with aesthetic philosophy. Kobayashi raises
the following issue: "The various and sundry explanations of Chang Ping-lin as either progressive or con-
servative are actually based on his political activities.
But in so far as they do not clarify what sustained
these activities--those aspects of human existence which
precede action--aren't those historical evaluations incomplete and arbitrary?"

We also have Sugiyama Fumihiko's essay, "T'an Ssu-
t'ung and his Dynastic World View"[a] (Hitotsubashi ronsō
81.3), which discusses T'an Ssu-t'ung from the perspective of his absolute principle of i-t'ai. Furthermore,
Takenaka Hiroaki's article, "On Late Ch'ing Knowledge
of Asia"[a] (Yasuda gakuen kenkyū kiyō 19), and Satō
Shin'ichi's "The Formation of Late Ch'ing Enlightenment
Thought: The Changing Appearance of the World"[a] (Kokka
gakkai zasshi 92.5-6, 93.1-2) touch on the reformers'
and the revolutionaries' knowledge of Asia and their
knowledge of the world, respectively.

Finally, there have been a number of book-length
works published over the past year: Masuda Wataru,
Seigaku Tōzen to Chūgoku jijō (The Eastern Movement of
Western Learning and Conditions in China)[a]; Ajia gendai-
shi I: Teikoku shugi no jidai (Contemporary Asian
History I: The Age of Imperialism); and Ajia gendaishi
II: Minzoku undō no hatten no jidai (Contemporary Asian
History II: The Age of the Development of Nationalist
Movements); Nakamura Tadashi, Shingai kakumei shi ken-
kyū (Studies in the History of the 1911 Revolution),[a]

see the review of this book by Yokoyama Hiroaki in
Shakai keizai shigaku 45.3); and Ono Ichirō, ed., Ryō
taisenken ki no Ajia to Nihon (Asia and Japan Between
the Two World Wars)[a]. There are also several essays
by Kōzuma Takae in Tō-A keizai kenkyū (46.3-4), which
give an overview of the modern and contemporary eras.
These are all worthy of serious book reviews.

Source materials and secondary studies from China
have been published recently in ever greater numbers,
and there have been opportunities for scholarly ex-
changes with Chinese scholars, such as Liu Ta-nien,
Wu Ch'eng-ming, Chang K'ai-Yüan, Fu I-ling, Huang
I-feng, Yen Chung-p'ing, and Ts'ai Mei-piao, all of
whom have visited Japan. One product of this exchange
can be seen in the following works: Kojima Shinji,
"Participating in the Scholarly Symposium on the History
of the Taiping Rebellion"[a] (Chūgoku kenkyū geppō 380);
Namiki Yorihisa , "On the Nature of the Taiping Regime:
A Debate at the 'Scholarly Symposium on the History of
the Taiping Rebellion'"[a] (Chūgoku kenkyū geppō 380);
Hazama Naoki, "Recent Chinese Studies of the May Fourth
Movement"[a] (Chūgoku kenkyū geppō 380); and Hazama Naoki,
"The Present State of Research Groups in China on the
1911 Revolution and Publication Plans for Studies and
Sources Relating to 1911: A Conversation with Chang
K'ai-yüan, Director of the 1911 Revolution Study
Group"[b] (Chūgoku kenkyū geppō 383).

MING-CH'ING STUDIES IN JAPAN: 1980
Wada Masahiro, in
Shigaku zasshi 90.5
(May 1981), 203-10.

In 1980 Japanese scholars published more than
seventy articles in the field of Ming-Ch'ing history;
these articles reflect a strong concern for the study
of water conservancy communities (suiri kyōdōtai) and
the nature of the gentry (kyōshin ron). I begin with
the debate (now nearing a climax) between Fujii Hiroshi
and Kusano Yasushi over the date when cultivation rights
for tenant farmers were firmly established in China; I
have therefore been forced to dispense with many essays
on other topics. The selection surely reflects a certain bias on the reviewer's part. Last year there were
quite a number of articles by Chinese scholars carried
in Japanese journals and there was an active scholarly
exchange (for example, the [Japanese] Ming-Ch'ing socio-
economic history delegation that visited Peking, Nanking, and Shanghai in April, and the international symposium on Ming-Ch'ing history held in Tientsin in
August). These meetings gave Chinese, Japanese, and
other foreign scholars the opportunity to deepen their
understanding of research problems. We would like to
see the concrete results of these sessions. We would
also like to see future opportunities for scholarly
exchange limited not merely to a privileged group of
scholars but opened up to the lower ranks of academia.

The Fujii-Kusano Debate
[Translator's note: In the following lengthy

discussion of the debate between Fujii and Kusano, the
author assumes knowledge of the outline of Fujii's long
article which has been published serially in Kindai Chūgoku during the past few years (beginning in 1979) and
which is still incomplete. I have therefore translated
in full in Appendix A the outline that appeared in Kindai Chūgoku 5 (April 1979). As of early 1984, the ninth
part of Fujii's article had been published and it covers
through II.B of the outline below. Altogether, the
essay is already nearly 600 pages in length.]

    Fujii Hiroshi's essay, "A New Study of the Story
'Shih-yüan chieh-yin,' in the Ch'uo-keng lu: An Explanation of the Term Chuan-chih"[b] (Tōhōgaku 59), is a
sister piece to his major work, "The Basic Structure
of the One-Field Two-Owners System (Part 3),"[a] (Kindai
Chūgoku 7). The former tries to explain the character
chih in the expression chuan-chih, which appears in the
"Shih-yüan chieh-yin" story. This story was originally
included in T'ao Tsung-i's Ch'uo-keng lu, and Fujii
claims that it was written on the basis of facts from
the early years of the Yüan dynasty in the early 14th
century. He presents a critical investigation of the
theory long held by scholars (including himself) that
chih had to do with pawning. He now argues that it
meant security money and concludes that chuan-chih
implied making someone else shoulder the burden of a
bond or security.

    This is his explanation of the following story,
[from the "Shih-yüan chieh-yin"-JAF]. Although tenant
farmer Ssu Ta gave to landlord Ch'en a certain amount
of money as a bond or chih, when the landlord dispos-
sessed Ssu of the land, he did not return the security
but compelled Li Ch'ing-ssu [to whom Ch'en had now
rented the land--JAF] to do so. Thus Ssu acquired the
right to claim from Li the return of the specified sum
of money, i.e., "repayment money" (so-ch'ou ch'ien)

known as <u>kuo-chung chih ch'ien</u>, or <u>chih</u>. With the money
received from Li, Ssu paid off his unpaid rent and used
the remaining sum as capital to open a wine shop.

    In other words, landlord Ch'en, distrustful of the
balance between the rent which Ssu was obliged to pay
and the bond Ssu had posted, tried on his own to have
Ssu transfer cultivation of the land to someone else
[i.e., Li]. This [transfer (<u>chuan</u>) of a bond (<u>chih</u>)]
was termed <u>chuan-chih</u> because the transaction necessarily involved the transfer of the obligation of returning
the bond to another person. Thus, <u>chuan-chih</u> can be
understood as repayment of what was in effect a capital
bond (of a fixed amount, but often without an established contractual form) for leased land (<u>tsu-t'ien</u>)
that the landlord had subsequently transferred to someone else.

    Therefore, Kusano Yasushi's argument[1] that <u>chuan-</u>
<u>chih</u> was the oldest extant example of surface rights on
private land is rejected, and Fujii holds fast to his
own view[1a] that the <u>chuan-chih</u> transaction between Ssu
and Li was wholly non-binding and had to accord with
the desires of the landlord. Not only does it not
illustrate the firm establishment of cultivation rights
for Ssu and Li, but furthermore it is not an example of
established cultivator rights among the wider tenant
farmer group at the time.

    Fujii's "The Basic Structure of the One-Field Two-
Owners System (part 3)"[a] is an analysis and critique
covering section II.A.1 of his overall outline. Prior
to his analysis of the <u>Ch'uo-keng lu</u> story, for about
half of this installment of the article, he marshalls
historical materials primarily from the Republican
period, when "surface rights" were fully developed,
and suggests eight different origins of "surface rights"
(in the larger sense) that existed during the latter
half of the Ch'ing, and particularly from the late

Ch'ing into the Republic. One of his examples from the
earlier period was the existence in Foochow during the
Wan-li reign of a one-field two-owners system that had
taken shape by legal prescription. Another is a record
of 1571 concerning land in the "Treatise on Rent and
Corvée" in chuan 5 of the Wan-li Chang-chou fu-chih,
which speaks of a one-field two-owners system (with a
division of the landlord's right to collect rent) and
a one-field three-owners system (with a division of the
landlord's right to collect rent and the tenant's right
of perpetual lease), both having taken shape through
false land registration in order to evade taxes (kui-
chi). From these Fujii infers that the formation of
the one-field two-owners system became a great social
problem in the period from the military upheavals of
the Chia-ching reign (1522-66) to the Lung-ch'ing era
(1567-72).

The analysis and critique of the Ch'uo-keng lu
story deals with a case arising from tenant land reclamation, namely the formative period for tenant labor
investment in the land, that indicated that the wages
and expenses that tenant farmers invested in improvement (reclamation, fertilization, and water utilization) of landlord-owned land. In this segment of the
essay, which completes the argument of earlier sections,
Fujii investigates in depth the historical sources in
order to refute each of the contradictions he sees in
Kusano's articles.

He also reanalyzes the entry on the land in the
"Treatise on Personages" in chuan 2 of the Chia-ching
Lung-kan hsien-chih. This passage recounts how the old
custom of making an advance payment to the landlord of
a bond (chih) developed into a form of private traffic
in cultivation rights (surface rights in a broad sense)
during the Chia-ching era. Fujii introduces data on
the practice of fen-chih-t'ien, an old institution

similar to chuan-chih still in effect in the Tung-
chiang region of the upper reaches of the Pei River in
Kwangtung during the Republican era. From these facts,
Fujii also is "forced to recognize that security money
itself, as well as tenant labor investment, was one of
the basic driving forces behind the acquisition of
surface rights for tenants." However, in conjunction
with stories from the late Yüan, he uses examples of
the extreme selfishness of landlords of that time to
refute the contradictory points that are in no way
explained by Sōda [Hiroshi's] and Kusano's theories,
which claim that Ssu Ta's transactions were being
carried out under conditions in which cultivator rights
for tenants at that time were widely established; why
then was it so easy for landlord Ch'en to divest Ssu,
against Ssu's will, of such established cultivator
rights and to rent the land to Li, a man he had picked
himself?

        In the fourth part of his article (Kindai Chūgoku
8), Fujii discusses section II.A.2 of the general outline. Prior to his analysis of ch'eng-chia,[2] he spends
nearly two-thirds of this essay demonstrating that the
Hung-wu Emperor's order of 1391, which stipulated categories of taxation for ch'i-chuang-hu[3] on ch'i-chuang
land, remained in effect throughout the Ming. (This
essay complements the argument in Fujii's earlier essay,
"The Origins of the One-Field Two-Owners System on
Ch'ung-ming Island,"[d] Tōhōgaku 49, [1975]). He criticizes
Kusano's theory, which asserts that the formation of
tenant's (i.e., surface) rights accompanied capital
amortization on Sung dynasty government lands, by supporting the theory of Takahashi Yoshirō, which argued
that the "value assigned in the transfer of tenancy
rights (li-chia chiao-tien)[4] and the buying or selling
of tenancy rights on government lands in the Sung[5] was
not considered to be capital but to be the value of the

land itself." Kusano tries also to trace the origins
of mai-chia and ch'eng-chia to the departmental bureaucratic apparatus on Ch'ung-ming Island in the year
1277 of the early Yuan. [By contrast] Fujii's
assertion in the Tōhōgaku article is to reiterate that
this is an error that derives from Kusano's misuse of
the two items that he used as sources for that period:
(1) the entry on the land in chuan 4 of the K'ang-hsi
Ch'ung-ming hsien-chih; and (2) the entry on the land
system in the "Treatise on Rent and Corvée" in chuan
4 of the Ch'ien-lung Chung-ming hsien-chih.

The term ch'eng-chia (the right of disposal of,
cultivation on, and earnings from the land gained
through the tenant's investment of labor) cannot be
traced back before Wan-li 32 (1604); it then appears as
pan-ch'eng-chia (there is no substantive evidence of
the meaning of this term). Its first appearance in the
expression mai-chia ch'eng-chia occurred eighty or
ninety years earlier (in the Cheng-te reign) in
Changsha. There is a difference in the content of mai-
chia ch'eng-chia between the two gazetteers which enables us to compare surface rights. In the K'ang-hsi
edition (printed 1681), ch'eng-chia did not confer
upon tenants the right to dispose of land, but in the
Ch'ieng-lung edition (printed 1760) ch'eng-chia did
allow tenants to dispose of land with the condition
that the landlord had the right of first refusal.

In cases where tenants were unable to obtain complete ch'eng-chia but only for labor investment in such
things as polder construction, they made up the rest
with t'ou-sheng-yin (budgeting silver). Complete
ch'eng-chia was thus attained; the combined sum of
[limited] ch'eng-chia and t'ou-sheng-yin for improvements resulting from labor investment constituted the
substance of complete ch'eng-chia. Thus, when a tenant
farmer sold his ch'eng-chia or surface rights on the

land which complete ch'eng-chia brought into existence,
there arose an obligation in principle on the part of
the new tenant to pay the former tenant a combined sum
for both [(limited) ch'eng-chia and t'ou-sheng-yin].
In such cases the t'ou-sheng-yin was called kuo-t'ou-
yin. However, in cases where the tenant sold surface
rights on land for which polder construction was fin-
ished and which had been made arable, neither the
value of the labor investment nor the t'ou-sheng-yin
had any real meaning as such for the new tenant, and
the combined sum of money was considered by the new
tenant simply as a bond [which he would get back when
he sold the land]. Kusano (in a 1977 article[b]) says
that during the late Ming-early Ch'ing a transformation
occurred on Ch'ung-ming Island from land on which the
tenant had invested his labor to kuo-t'ou land--in
other words, kuo-t'ou land witnessed a "deterioration
and decline" in surface practices "after the Ming-
Ch'ing transition." What Kusano calls kuo-t'ou land,
Fujii refers to as bond (ya-chin) land or ting-shou
land, and he concludes that by paying a large amount
of ting-shou, the tenant obtained surface rights.[6]

With his essay, "The Degeneration of Surface
Rights in the Late Ming and Early Ch'ing: The Case of
the Fukien-Kiangsu-Kwangtung Border Region"[c] (Kumamoto
daigaku bungakubu ronsō-shigaku hen 1), Kusano presents
a part of his argument in response to Fujii's [notion
of the bond-rent relationship, discussed above].[6a]
Kusano concludes that the struggle that developed
between landlord and tenant in the mountainous Fukien-
Kiangsi-Kwangtung border area in the late Ming and
early Ch'ing was not a peasant fight over the establishment of a topsoil system (at the point of its
formation), but rather was a dispute that arose over
the aggression of landlords who were trying to elim-
inate the framework for the bond-rent (ya-tsu) relation-

ship. According to Kusano, the complaint of tenant
farmers heard from the Ch'ung-chen era (1628-44) through
the Ch'ien-lung era in the latter half of the 18th
century was: "We create the land and clear the land;
we can be banished from it but cannot sell it." Tenants particularly opposed the reinstitution of contracts
through which small cultivators leased land for a fixed
period of time. These contracts, known as huan-p'i
(buying cultivation, transferring cultivation, and
selling a lease--called soyaku kōkan by Kusano), was
antithetical to the system of topsoil rights and sig-
nalled its impending collapse. Kusano finds an explanation for why landlords could implement fixed term
leases in the decrease in the number of people working
the land because of the new development of arable
mountain land. [Since tenants were leaving to claim
and cultivate mountain land on their own,] the old topsoil system was being submerged in a [new] system of
bond-rent lands (ya-tsu-t'ien) [that did not confer any
surface rights] and was losing its essence as a system
of topsoil rights. He claims that "this practice of
fixed term leases was not something that ultimately
could be accepted by that tenant (i.e., topsoil-working)
stratum who had long lived peacefully with the old topsoil system."

   At the same time, however, Kusano notes in the
"Letter to Magistrate Li" (which is included in chuan
8 of the Wei Li Wei Chi-tzu wen-chi) that: "The local
people tilled the fields, and all were from Fukien. . .
There was an uprising in the Southeast, and the bandits
eyed the city. They said that if we did not give in,
they would destroy [the system of] the tenant farmers.
We [quoth the "bandits," actually peasant rebels--JAF]
shall reform your age-old custom of the past several
hundred years." This citation, he argues, contradicts
"the fact that those who worked the topsoil were letting

it be known that with the support of their own 'troops
off the land,' they had reached an understanding with
the local officials about the preservation of past topsoil practices." However, surely the "age-old custom
of several hundred years" which "we" (i.e., the topsoil
workers) announced they would "reform" for the tenant
farmers was the fixed-term leases, which even Kusano
recognizes were never accepted by the tenant (topsoil-
working) stratum. In other words, the elimination of
landlord fixed-term leases was tied to the establishment of topsoil rights for the tenant farmers. In
addition, the examples Kusano raises from Hsing-kuo
county over the years 1673-1726 and from Jui-chin
county in 1729 indicate that the abolition of fixed-
term leases was partially realized in the 18th century.
        In short, there is a major difference between
Fujii and Kusano in their evaluations of the cultivation (i.e., topsoil) rights of tenants. Fujii finds
the beginnings of a system of topsoil rights in the
latter half of the Ming, its formation and establishment from the mid-Ch'ing on (especially from the late
Ch'ing into the Republic), and finally its dissolution
with the founding of the People's Republic of China.
Kusano sees topsoil practices "forming in the Sung,
flourishing from the Yüan into the Ming, then beginning
to fall into decline after the late Ming and early
Ch'ing. During the Republican era with the compilation
of a modern civil code, topsoil customs finally headed
toward their end." We shall keep a watch on the changes
in this debate.

Systems of Property Ownership

        In his essay, "From the Kuan-t'ien shih-mo k'ao to
the 'Su-Sung erh-fu t'ien-fu chih chung': Ku Yen-wu
and Local Land Problems in Soochow and Sung-chiang in
the Early Ch'ing"[g] (Nagoya daigaku Tōyōshi kenkyū

hōkoku 6), Mori Masao does a comparative analysis of:
(1) hsien-k'e-i (a curtailment of the rate of tax
assessment) which appears in the appendix to the last
volume of the Kuan-t'ien shih-mo k'ao, which served as
Ku Yen-wu's work notes for his "Su-Sung erh-fu t'ien-
fu chih chung" located in chuan 10 of the Jih-chih lu;
and (2) the last fourteen lines of the "Su-Sung erh-fu
t'ien-fu chih chung." As a result of his analysis,
Mori discovered a significant change in terminology
from "those who tilled the land themselves were few" in
the earlier text [i.e., the appendix] to "those who
owned the land were one in ten" in the latter [essay on
Soochow and Sung-chiang]. [He interprets] this change
as indicating severe criticism by Ku Yen-wu of concentration of land ownership in the hands of landlords
because it contributed to the extraordinary impoverishment of cultivator peasants. Because the liability for
taxes and corvée formed the basis for the exploitation
of tenant labor, Mori tries to detect common points
between[, on the one hand,] Ku Yen-wu's position, which
stressed the urgent need for immediate rent reduction
by curtailing the rate of tax assessment, and [on the
other,] the [Ch'ing] state's policy evident by the late
Yung-cheng reign of protecting tenants in their relations with landlords.

Ihara Kōsuke's article, "The Management of Property in Land by Shih-jen in the Late Ming and Early
Ch'ing: The Case of Chang Lü-hsiang's Family"[a] (in
Shigaku ronsō) analyzes from the perspective of the
social relations of a shih-jen, i.e. sheng-yüan, the
actual conditions of management on the roughly fifty
mou of land owned by the Chang family. Ihara shows
clearly that the downfall of the Changs was due to the
interaction of their dual role as managers and as landlords.[7]

Yamana Hirofumi's essay, "Charitable Estates in

Kiangnan in the Late Ch'ing"[a] (Tōyō gakuhō 62.1-2),
investigates the character of late Ch'ing landlordism
as manifested in the revival of land ownership and the
guarantee of rent collection after the Taiping Rebellion. He does so by looking at the charitable estate
lands held together by the clan cohesion of city-
dwelling landlords in the Soochow area.

Water Conservancy Communities

     In his essay, "A Study of Yeh-shih tien-li,"[b]
(Tōyōshi kenkyū 39.1), Hamashima Atsutoshi analyzes
the water conservancy system called yeh-shih tien-li
from the perspective of its qualitative development
since the Sung. He looks at the overall administration
of water conservancy by Keng Chü, county magistrate of
Ch'ang-shu [Kiangsu], from about 1602-07. Yeh-shih
implied that the landlords provided the provisions; and
tien-li meant that tenants provided the raw labor.
Hamashima singles out two points for analysis: (a)
the supplementing of opportunities for tenant farmers
to obtain money (or work hours) by simple production of
goods (household handicrafts) was taken away from them
by Keng Chü in the sense that he paid them in grains;
and (b) the enforcement by dynastic authority of guar-
anteeing the labor of tenant farmers who held the
capacity, even more advantageous than that of dredging
and constructing dikes, to say "no." In these two ways,
he claims, yeh-shih tien-li in the late Ming marked a
qualitative difference in the means by which tenant
farmers maintained a margin of physical subsistence
[above the farming level], as compared with the famine
conditions in the time of Fan Chung-yen in the Sung.
     Hamashima's essay, "Several Perspectives on Polders
in Kiangnan"[c] (Tōdaishi kenkyūkai hōkoku III) represents
one of the results for the Ming-Ch'ing period from the
project on historical research into villages and popu-

lation centers in China. The following new observation
of his is worthy of our attention: "The unit of organization for rent resistance that took the form of lien-
yü chieh-chia [solidarity across polder boundaries] was
the village. The cohesion of a village formed the basis
for rent resistance, and the village was often a center
of population that was situated on the bank of a creek
and cut across polder boundaries. The lands cultivated
by the inhabitants of such villages were united by being
adjacent to each other (although borders remained unclear) and possessed a specific space that included
scattered polders." He presents this argument with
tables and charts rich in informative material including a diagram of polder lands.

In his essay, "Cotton Production and Water Utilization in the Yangtze Delta, Late Ming to Early Ch'ing
(2)"[a] (Kyūshū daigaku Tōyōshi ronshū 8), Kawakatsu
Mamoru tries to show, although still unsuccessfully,
that the development of cotton production was one cause
of the destruction of water control in Kiangnan, even
though local gazetteers from the T'ai-ts'ang region in
the late Ming report that the ruination of water control caused the growth of cotton production and that
landlords had to coerce their tenants into rice production. He tries to interpret tenant farmers' strategies
in terms of developing their productive capacities by
diversified cultivation of cotton and soybeans in
response to landlord expropriations.

Oh Keum-sung, in his essay "The Development of
Water Utilization and Village Society around Lake Tung-
t'ing in the Late Ming"[a] (translated by Yamane Yukio,
Chūgoku suirishi kenkyū 10) proposes first that a small
number of non-degree-holding landlords and gentry controlled the productive functions of the "community,"
exemplified in the management of the restoration of
water utilization facilities around Lake Tung-t'ing in

Hunan in the late Ming. He denies the existence of an
extremely bifurcated rice-cultivating village society
by looking at cases of remarkable upward social mobility
among the local peasantry and at a growing number of
sojourners, revealing a very complex [social situation].
Oh also points out that there were normally quite a
number of owner-cultivator peasants.

   In his essay, "Water Conservancy Customs in Kiangnan in the Ch'ing Dynasty and the Hsiang-tung System"[c]
(Shirin 63.1), Ōtani Toshio points out that from the
mid-Ch'ing on the increase of tax payments for waterworks and the establishment of the hsiang-tung system
meant the strengthening of official supervisory powers
over those water conservancy projects funded through
popular capital accumulation (min-pien) based on the
yeh-shih tien-li model [see discussion of Hamashima's
article[b] above]. He also says that the manager responsible for water conservancy was not filling a revived
corvée position from the past, but was undertaking a
[new kind of] job which shouldered tasks in one corner
of the local administrative apparatus.

   Morita Akira's essay, "The Ch'ing Policy of Water
Conservation and Field Cultivation[8] in the Capital
Region"[b] (Shakai bunka shigaku 18), begins from the
recent perspective of the increase in agricultural
productivity in North China brought about by the policy
of "transferring southern waters to the north" (nan-shui
pei-tiao), part of China's Four Modernizations. He
traces a policy lesson [for contemporary China to the
Ch'ing] when the structure of "transferring southern
tribute grain to the north" (nan-liang pei-tiao) (a
system itself the product of dual political and economic functions which separated the North and South,
respectively) dissolved into a larger form. Morita
then looks specifically at the policy of water conservation and field cultivation in the capital area

around Peking that underwent positive development during
the Ch'ing.

Debate on the Scope of Exchange Markets

In his essay, "Hsü and Shih in Kwangtung During
the Ming and Ch'ing Periods: A View of the Forms and
Functions of Traditional Markets"[a] (Shirin 63.1),
Hayashi Kazuo uses the abundant local gazetteers from
the Ming-Ch'ing period to analyze the relationship
between, on the one hand, the configuration and function of those markets that became secondary living
nexuses in Kwangtung province from the latter half of
the Ming on and, on the other, the society that supported those markets. He argues in particular that the
markets formed an economic unit that transcended villages because many markets were organized by gentry who
planned to accumulate wealth as well as to attain local
control. Products of the villagers in any given region
were bought up, and all the objects of daily use as well
as the necessities of life were supplied them. This
insight takes us quite a step forward in understanding
the connection between the formation of market areas
and local gentry control.[9]

Mizuni Masaaki, in his essay "On the Hsin-an
yüan-pan shih-shang lei-yao"[a] (Tōhōgaku 60), clearly
demonstrates that the original text of the work was
published in 1626, at the height of prosperity of
Huichow merchants in the late Ming, and that therefore
it contained entries on distances starting at Hsin-an,
unlike other merchant compendia that cite Nanking or
Fukien as points of departure. Because it was literally a handbook for scholars (shih) and merchants
(shang), and cannot simply be called a merchant manual,
this text illustrates social changes involving upward
social mobility of merchants and downward mobility of
scholars.

Legal History

Wada Masahiro has written two articles concerning
bureaucratic systems: "The Process of the Emergence of
Kuan-p'ing in the Late Ming"[d] (Kyūshū daigaku Tōyōshi
ronshū 8); and "The Process of the Emergence of Wo-
fang in the Late Ming"[e] (Tōyō gakuhō 62.1-2). The former discusses how kuan-p'ing, another expression for
k'ao-yü (investigative efficiency reports), arose from
the process in which those questioned in gathering information for k'ao-yü changed from being the local elders to being low-ranking officials. This change was
due to problems in making inquiries about keeping the
peace, as they related to assessment of administrative
achievement, a job which was the responsibility of
local officials from the Chia-ching reign onward. The
latter essay examines one aspect of the circumstances
under which yamen runners (ya-i) who emerged from the
practice of delegated tsao-li[10]), acting in their capacity to "investigate secrets" (wo-fang) as a group,
privatized kuan-p'ing inquiries.

Two essays were published concerning military
systems: Okuyama Norio, "A Study of Capital Garrisons
in the Mid-Ming"[a] (Mindaishi kenkyū 8); and Aoyama
Jirō, "On Capital Garrisons in the Chia-ching Reign of
the Ming Dynasty"[a] (Sundai shigaku 49). Okuyama demonstrates the decline in status of meritorious officials
(hsün-ch'en) and generals (chiang-ling) in the capital
garrison power structure from the Ch'eng-hua through
the Chia-ching reigns of the Ming and the shift in
military authority toward the court officialdom and the
Board of War. Aoyama shows the decline of capital garrisons was due primarily to the impoverishment of the
ying-chün and pan-chün, which in turn was caused by the
structural reforms made in the capital garrison system
in the Chia-ching reign and the cooptation and exploitation of military officials.

In the field of labor service systems, we have two
essays: Satō Manabu, "On the Problem of Corvée Exemption
for Merchants in the Capital in the Late Ming"[a] (Shūkan
Tōyōgaku 44); and Meguro Katsuhiko, "On the Pao-chia
System in the Mid-Ch'ing Period: The Case of P'ing-hu
County, Chekiang in the Chia-ch'ing Era"[b] (Aichi kyōiku
daigaku kenkyū hōkoku--shakai kagaku 29). The first article illuminates the problem of the evasion of labor
service by powerful merchants. To do this, Satō analyzes the development of urban industry from the middle
of the Ming on and points to the contradiction spawned
by the exactions of the feudal state vis à vis this
growth. As a result, Satō demonstrates that in order to
control the merchants, which ideally the state should
have done in an equitable manner, eunuchs were used as
intermediaries and they in fact illegally assumed the
power of giving out exemptions for labor service. In
this capacity, they functioned entirely differently
towards powerful merchants than they did towards middle
or small merchants.

In the latter essay Meguro argues that a peculiar
condition existed in P'ing-hu county where there was
extensive participation in the pao-chia system by the
local gentry because the breakdown in systems to maintain public order had been revealed in the progress of
the crushing of the White Lotus rebels. As a means of
preserving order, cumulative inspection registers known
as ling-hu ts'e were additionally instituted. In an
effort to avoid the burden and responsibility, the
local gentry forced the ti-pao to take over management
of these registers. Work remains to be done on whether
the local elders were completely excluded from all
pao-chia duties. In this regard we need to wait for a
separate review of Kawakatsu Mamoru's major work,
Chūgoku hōken kokka no shihai kōzō: Min-Shin fueki
seido shi no kenkyū (The ruling structure of the feudal

state in China: A study of the history of taxation and
service systems in the Ming and Ch'ing dynasties).[d]

On the Nature of the Gentry

Yamane Yukio and Inada Hideko have translated an
essay by the Korean scholar Oh Keum-sung, "On the Formative Process of the Shen-shih Class in the Ming (1)"[b]
(Mindaishi kenkyū 8). In this part of his essay, Oh
argues that after the early Ming the regulations for exemption from labor service for sheng-yüan, who quali-
fied as members of the privileged strata for life by
virtue of passing the examinations, first appear in an
entry in the Veritable Records of the Ming Dynasty
dated Hung-wu 20 (1387), 10th month, ting-mao day. The
regulations for chien-sheng and chü-jen (which first
appear in 1405 in the entries under tien-chih (hsia),
tz'u-yü, and fu-yu in chüan 2 of the Wang-ts'ai Huang-
Ming t'ai-hsüeh chih) are, however, in fact comparable
to those promulgated for sheng-yüan in 1387.

The essay, "The Equitable Field-Equitable Labor
System (chün-t'ien chün-i) and the Local Gentry of the
Late Ming and Early Ch'ing (2): Chu Kuo-chen's 'Letter
to Great Grandfather and Great Grandmother'"[d] (Shihō
11), is the second part of Hamashima Atsutoshi's study
of the local gentry. He begins with reference to the
gentry involvement in chün-t'ien chün-i. In response
to Okuzaki Yūji and Kawakatsu Mamoru, who have criti-
cized his work, Hamashima reaffirms the theory that:
(a) the emergence of Chu Kuo-chen, whose father had
been a hard-laboring small landowner, was one of the
decisive reasons for this political movement [to equalize tax and labor service burdens] ; (b) Chu was never
a large landlord; and (c) Chu was completely opposed
to exempting criminals from labor for illness or other
excuses (t'ieh-i)[11] and advocated the retention of
assigned labor duties (tang-i).[12]

Fuma Susumu's article, "Riots of Scholars Against
Local Officials in the Late Ming"[a] (Tōhō gakuhō 52),
analyzes the sheng-yüan riots that broke out in various
places mainly in Kiangnan from the Wan-li to the Ch'ung-
chen reigns of the late Ming. He argues that these
riots took the form of rent resistance supported by the
local gentry "assembly" (kung-i)[13]which advocated the
righteousness of the [rioters'] cause. They humiliated
and chased the county magistrates from office, and re-
fused to behave as they were expected to. Why were the
local elders excluded from the local gentry "assembly"?

Yamamoto Eiji's essay, "On Village Headmen in
T'ien-t'ai County, Chekiang: A Look at Local Village
Control in China in the Early 18th Century"[a] (Shigaku
50), presents the data through which he analyzes the
function and nature, as well as the abuses and their
causes, of village headmen (t'u-t'ou), the resident
village functionaries who frequently took part in T'ien-
t'ai politics. He also locates the essence of local
gentry control in those sheng-yüan and chien-sheng who
made use of t'u-t'ou assignments.

In his essay "Local Gentry in the Ming Dynasty:
Notes on the Connection Between the Literati and Local
Society"[h] (Nagoya daigaku bungakubu kenkyū ronshū 26),
Mori Masao posits two types of local gentry on the
basis of their intentions with respect to local society,
i.e. the county: (1) those concerned with statecraft
(ching-shih chi-min) [i.e., good government] ; and (2)
those concerned with rising in office in order to get
rich (sheng-kuan fa-ts'ai). He discusses the significance of the existence of the first type in terms of
their responsibility toward local society. How would
Mori deal with the fact that local elders, who are not
to be found in local gentry "assemblies" according to
Fuma's article, do show up in the local gentry "assemblies" in the K'ang-hsi and Yung-cheng reigns?

Political History

In his essay "Currency Policy During the Ming Period"[b] (Tōyōshi kenkyū 39.3), Danjō Hiroshi locates the political importance of the government's policy regarding the circulation of paper currency in the early Ming as part of the North-South problem in Chinese history. He argues that, in conjunction with the political centralization of power after the capital was moved to Peking, a recovery policy was implemented with the issuance of "Great Ming paper currency" (Ta Ming pao-ch'ao), a policy whose purpose was the centralization of economic power. These new paper bills were non-exchangeable and no reserves were on hand for their conversion. This policy was designed to gain economic control over Kiangnan, which the central government feared would make itself self-sufficient through silver circulation.

Taniguchi Kikuo's article, "On Ch'en Yu-liang's State of Ta-han"[b] (Tōyōshi kenkyū 39.1), uses the activities of those influential leaders who supported Ch'en Yu-liang's [14th century] regime as a way of analyzing the causes of Ch'en's defeat in his struggle with Chu Yüan-chang and the rapid collapse of his power. Taniguchi recognizes the existence of followers of the White Lotus sect in Hsü Shou-hui's group, the Western Red Army (Hsi-hsi hung-chün) as well as in Ch'en Yu-liang's group, but his position differs from that of Sōda Hiroshi.

In his essay, "The Li-chia System in T'ai-tsu's Political Engineering: On the Writings of the Fang-chin yü-shih"[a] (Tōdaishi kenkyūkai hōkoku III), Hosono Kōji maintains that the system of elders (lao-jen), which commenced about the same time as the li-chia system, developed by stages from the ch'i-su system, to the hsiang-lao system, to the li-lao system. He regards the system of elders as a policy designed to control

decadent officials who feared that village society would
be led into a crisis under the li-chia system, itself
the economic basis for the firm establishment of Ming
T'ai-tsu's regime. There remain several lingering
problems in this essay, such as: Isn't what Hosono
calls the hsiang-lao just another name for li-lao?

Ono Kazuko's essay, "A Study of the Tung-lin
Clique (1)"[a] (Tōhō gakuhō 52), argues that when Ku Hsien-
ch'eng was its ideologue the Tung-lin clique dealt in a
merciful manner with those issues of secondary moral
importance concerning Li San-ts'ai (who was attacked
for being a spendthrift and for taking bribes). They
sought to locate in Li's specific case the capacity to
realize kung, that is their political morality or local
"popular" opinion. We would like to know the class content of Ono's notion of "popular."

Class Relations

Sōda Hiroshi's essay, "A Study of the Red Turbans:
The Tradition of Popular Armed Groups in China"[b]
(Tōyōshi kenkyū 38.4), looks at the "Red Turban" tradition that had its roots in the popular armed bands that
were active in much of Hupeh, Kiangsu, and Anhwei
during the transition from Northern to Southern Sung.
He raises several points of interest with respect to
their role in popular uprisings, their internal cohesion
and group structure, the changes they underwent as they
met resistance, and their projection as a class in the
Shui-hu chuan. He claims that the Red Turbans from the
Red Turban Army of the late Yüan were a well-armed group
that should be distinguished from the White Lotus
religion.

Itō Kimio's essay, "A Reinvestigation of Pirate
Rebellions in the Chia-ching Era: On Wang Chih and the
Pirate Rebellions of the 1550's"[a] (Mindaishi kenkyū 8),
is based on Sakuma Shigeo's theory, and is critical of
Katayama Seijirō's argument that the pirate rebellions

of the 1550's were class conflicts. Itō argues that
exploitation by the gentry sufficient to make the independence of small and middle merchants a necessity did
not exist; and that it is difficult to pinpoint the relationship between Wang Chih and the pirate rebellions
of the third decade of the Chia-ching reign on the
basis of a critique of the sources, such as the Ch'ou-
hai t'u-pien. The discovery of new materials is to be
hoped for.

    Feng Erh-k'ang's essay, "Yung-cheng's Elimination
of Beggars as a Registration Category in Shao-hsing and
Ch'ang-shu"[a] (Shūkan Tōyōgaku 44), argues that one can
evaluate the Yung-cheng Emperor's order for the release
of kai-hu [local "mean" people] from the registers as
leading to an increase in the productive capacity of
the population. Yet the feudal economic structure and
economic life (to say nothing of its strictly ranked
systems and hierarchical mode of thought) continued to
exist for kai-hu who were burdened with unremunerative
corvée labor services to the ruling class. [Their "emancipation"] was merely an ordinance, because at the time
such an occupational changeover was impossible. Feng
claims that their true liberation would have to await
the establishment of the new China two hundred years
later.

    Kobayashi Kazumi's article, "The Character of the
White Lotus Rebellion of the Chia-ch'ing Era"[a] (in
Nakajima ronshū, vol. 1), seeks to locate the sensitiv-
ity surrounding the resuscitation of concepts [by members of the White Lotus sect] that were symbolic of the
spiritual structure of the White Lotus movement: deform-
ity, silence, sacrifice, suicide upon the death of one's
superior, obedience, vengeance, and eros.

    In his essay, "An Effort to Understand the White
Lotus Movement Touched off by the Debate over Millenarian Movements"[b] (in Nakajima ronshū, vol. 1), Noguchi

Tetsurō regards the White Lotus sect as different from other religions. He tries to see the side of it that resembled the character of the millenarian movements in the Middle Ages in Western Europe.

International Relations

Yoshida Kin'ichi's essay, "On Russian Ambassador Spathari's Mission to China"[a] (Shigaku zasshi 89.11), is a painstaking effort to elucidate in concrete terms the trends exhibited in the earliest formal diplomatic disputes between the two feudal empires of China and Russia surrounding the resolution of border conflicts over sovereignty in Heilungkiang in the latter half of the 17th century. This study is based on rich historical materials such as memorials in the Manchu language. He draws fascinating connections with the contemporary problems of these two nations in their currect negotiations.

Yoshida has also written "The Chart of the Nine Rivers of Chi-lin of Lang T'an and the Treaty of Nerchinsk" (Tōyō gakuhō 62.1-2) in which he fixes 1690 (K'ang-hsi 29) as the date of completion of The Chart of the Nine Rivers of Chi-lin, a work that was very important to the Treaty of Nerchinsk.

Thought

In his essay, "On the Function of Li in Pre-Modern China"[c] (Hitotsubashi ronsō 83.4), Mizoguchi Yūzō criticizes the theory held by Morimoto Shun'ichirō and Iwama Kazuo on the feudal nature of Chu Hsi's concept of li. He presents a new thesis that in the time from Chu Hsi to Wang Yang-ming, the function of li was limited to a unitary hierarchic function whereby the virtuous sage and literati-officials demonstrated their moral nature by governing those beneath them. However, from Ming times on this pre-modern li served as China's characteristic principle of harmonious order for one's own and

others' wishes in social (that is, hierarchical) relations.

Mizoguchi has also written "The Development of the
Concepts of Public and Private in China"[d] (Shisō 669).
He traces how, through the period from the late 16th
century to the failure of the Taiping Rebellion, the
concept of "public" within the literati world was trans-
muted from the economic to the political sphere. He also points to the traditional lack of individuality that
characterizes "public" in both realms.

Literature

Isobe Akira's "A Study of the Readership of the
Hsi-yu chi in the Late Ming: The Problem of the Readers
of 'Classical Vernacular Fiction' in the Ming"[a] (Shūkan
Tōyōgaku 44) begins with a comparative investigation of
a day's pay for a laborer at the end of the Ming (about
thirty wen; totalling about 1.5 taels of silver per
month) and various commodity and book prices. In
denying previously held theories, Isobe shows that
classical novels were extraordinarily expensive items
of pleasure and cultivation; and that readers of the
Hsi-yu chi were the literati, members of the inner court,
imperial relatives, and rich merchants in the Wan-li
through Ch'ung-chen reigns.

APPENDIX A

Comprehensive Outline of Fujii Hiroshi's Essay,
"The Basic Structure of the One-Field Two-Owners System"

Introduction

I. The Basic Concept of the One-Field Two-Owners System

   A. The Meaning of the One-Field Two-Owners System

   B. The Meaning of Surface [Topsoil] Rights and
      Subsoil Rights

      1. Their Original Meanings

      2. Their Meanings as Generic Terms

II. The Evolution of the One-Field Two-Owners System

   A. Invested Tenant Labor and Surface Rights

      1. An Analysis and Critique of Ch'uo-keng lu
         Stories

      2. The Meaning of Ch'eng-chia on Ch'ung-ming
         Island

   B. Ting-shou and Surface Rights

   C. Relationship Between Surface Rights and Tsu-tien

III. Surface Rights and Perpetual Cultivation Rights

IV. The Spread of the One-Field Two-Owners System

V. The Decline of the One-Field Two-Owners System

VI. The Historical Significance of the One-Field
    Two-Owners System

Conclusion

JAPANESE STUDIES OF POST-OPIUM WAR CHINA: 1980
Namiki Yorihisa, in
Shigaku zasshi 90.5
(May 1981), 210-18.

It is now several years since the great upheavals
of the autumn of 1976, and China is fortifying its image
as an "ordinary nation." Our understanding of China is
confused because of the "realization" that in fact the
People's Republic is a society that is lagging behind.
There is a trend that can also be seen in the major
changes afoot in the field of modern Chinese history.
Since 1976 historical research has taken as its slogan
"seek truth through facts" (shih-shih ch'iu-shih) and
the "liberation of thought" (ssu-hsiang chieh-fang).
[There has been a change] from an emphasis on the continuous upsurge of the past revolution -- for example,
the mass of studies (due to the tempetuous post-'49
struggles between lines) on the lack of organization and
spontaneity of the Boxer Movement, which was then traced
to the "ignorant" struggle of the peasantry--to an emphasis on the bourgeois development toward capitalism
in China. Shake-ups of various kinds, now stimulating
China's transformation, are occurring in our method of
comprehending "modern" in our own studies of modern
Chinese history. Modern Chinese historical research,
which has long stood at the threshold, can now be said
to be undergoing a great transformation.

According to Banno Ryōkichi ("Ideas and Methods in
Modern Chinese Research: Reflections on Hatano [Yoshi-
hiro's] Historiography,"[a] Nagoya daigaku Tōyōshi kenkyū
hōkoku 6), in our present state of research, we "are at

a 'post-war' crossroads in relations with China and in
our understanding of China." Banno argues that "it
seems that modern Chinese historical studies are beginning to form one specialized area within the intellectual structure of world history." This is a result of
an ongoing development in postwar scholarship that began
in the decade after the 1949 Revolution when "an enthu-
siasm that attempted to unravel the secrets of rapid
progress toward an advanced China stimulated many scholars"; during the time of the Sino-Soviet conflict and
the Cultural Revolution, we passed through an era when
the "confidence in the supremacy of Chinese socialism
gradually receded, and the extraordinary social progress
of the past seemed to be stagnation, leading to a rupture in our understanding of China." We then moved into
a period in which we "have fallen into a confusion of
values, with doubts about Chinese socialism." As indicated by his subtitle, Banno takes as his point of departure the work of Hatano Yoshihiro, who caused a great
debate in the history of postwar research by "groping
for a method to confirm the impression that grim reality
had prescribed a distinctive nature to modern China," an
impression derived from his "realization that 'compared
to the modernization of Japan, China's modernization was
tardy and failing.'" Banno traces in detail the history
of research critical of Hatano's work and holds that the
critiques of Hatano "have been either incomplete or
flawed in form and method, and their arguments intellectually inconsistent and slack in the investigation of
their own principles." At the same time, much productive work has been accomplished, and Banno tries to provide an outline for the future reconstruction of modern
and contemporary Chinese history.

Postwar studies include a number of areas of debate. My impression -- shared by many people -- is
that they have not necessarily achieved their full pur-

pose by leading to further studies, but have rather
stimulated a dispersal of research interests. Yet,
Nozawa Yutaka ("Toward Progress in Research into Modern
and Contemporary Asian History (2),"[b] in Rekishi kagaku)
recognizes in his postscript that Banno's point about
Hatano is worth "paying heed to." In Nozawa's estima-
tion, "it is necessary to address as a crucial question
the view that postwar studies of China have reached a
turning point." He notes that, in reordering the debated
areas in the history of postwar scholarship, the skeletal
elements of the research have taken a vacillating course
and the contributions of those who have concentrated on
Chinese research in the postwar period have been unsatis-
factory. At the same time he cites Nakanishi Tsutomu
and Satoi Hikoshichirō as individuals who "with a wide
field of vision and an exacting focus have been able to
indicate with precision the location of problems." He
argues that: (1) the issues of research posture and
methodology, although providing important clues for the
continuation and development of postwar research, were
not deepened in the AF controversy,[1] which centered on
the critique of "modernization" theory; (2) the emotional
opposition spawned in the process of debate prevented
unity among "dedicated scholars"; and (3) the chasm had
a negative effect even into the Cultural Revolution
period. Nozawa also believes "modern and contemporary
Chinese historical studies to have finally gotten onto
the right track." With the passing of the Cultural
Revolution, China's "vacuous icons" were exploded, but
he does not explicitly mention work on the "debated
areas" in the period from the Cultural Revolution
through the 1970's.

By contrast, Ishida Yoneko deals directly with the
history of research on the 1911 Revolution in her essay
"Various Results of Recent Japanese Research on the 1911
Revolution"[a] (Tōyōshi kenkyū 39.1). She uses an issue

raised by Kobayashi Kazumi in the field of the history
of popular uprisings, and criticizes the accumulated,
would-be objective works of research for being "unclear
about just what they are trying to clarify and why."
"I should like to take as my problem" for consideration,
she argues, "the attempt to recover the living bond between ourselves today (the subjective element in research) and history, which is the creation of human
beings; and [I will] not attempt to see historical progress in the pre-established and formulaic ascendance of
historical stages, but will try and recover the meaning
of liberation and reconstruct its stages." She clarifies an insight into the essence of our contemporary research in modern Chinese history that is worthy of our
attention.

We can keenly sense through the above three essays
that the issues of what was and what is "modern" in China
-- in connection with various problems that are being revealed as the Chinese pursue "modernization" -- are again
being sharply directed at none other than those researchers among us in Japan.

Let us look at essays that deal with the development of capitalist production relations in modern China.
Suzuki Tomoo's "The Establishment of Shanghai's Mechanized
Textile Industry"[a] (Nakajima ronshū, vol. 1) criticizes
the following point of view. The establishment in
Shanghai of mechanized textile factories drew together
foreign and Chinese merchants, while hand-reeling production continued to retreat before the competition with
Japanese and Italian raw silk that had already existed
during Shanghai's industrial and investment booms of
about 1880. In the face of this situation, those among
Kiangsu and Chekiang raw silk merchants who could show
a profit by using the pre-existing system of exploitation concentrated on obstructing and restricting this
mechanization through certain Westernization (yang-wu)

policies. These policies included the reorganization
of the cocoon tax (chien-chüan), the regulation of
cocoon dealers (chien-hang), and the regulation of the
supply of raw cocoons, and formed the objective conditions for the development of capitalism. Instead,
Suzuki sees the relationship between foreign capital and
Chinese merchants in Shanghai, on the one hand, and the
Kiangsu-Chekiang raw silk merchants/Westernizers, on the
other, as an antagonistic one. He also believes that
the rapid development of the mechanized textile industry
actually became possible after the Sino-Japanese War,
when limitations were relaxed on foreign industrial
rights. It seems, however, that important problems
remain to be investigated relating to the specific
structure of earlier raw silk production and the previous system of exploitation, the relationship of
these structures to the Westernizing group, and the
social position of those Shanghai merchants who initial-
ly launched the mechanized textile industry.

Within a larger framework, problems concerning
mechanized textile production became one stage in the
overall process of both capitalist relations of production aimed at penetrating the domestic markets of Shanghai as well as in China's traditional economic system.
In this regard, there are two articles by Nakai Hideki:
"On the Chinese Cotton Spinning Industry in the Late
Ch'ing: A Reexamination of the Origin of the Depression
in Local Spinning"[a] (Hokkaidō daigaku jimbun kagaku
ronshū 16); and "The Management and Market Conditions
for the Cotton Spinning Industry in the Late Ch'ing:
The Place of the Dah Sun Cotton Mill in Local Chinese
Spinning"[b] (Shakai keizai shigaku 45.5). In these
essays Nakai reinvestigates the theory, commonly held
since Yen Chung-p'ing, that found the cause of the depression in late Ch'ing native spinning in the importation of foreign cotton thread and the pressure of the

foreign-capitalized spinning industry. He points out
the complex channels of management agencies and compradors through whom foreign-capitalized spinning products
had to pass in order to reach Chinese markets and enter
into fierce competition with Chinese cotton thread in
the Kiangnan delta (the center of native spinning).
Nakai stresses the fact that the economy generally could
not sustain modern economic activity as a condition for
checking the growth potential of native spinning. In
discussing Chang Chien, one of those transitional types
who appeared during the changeover from traditional to
modern society, Nakai stresses the role played by Chang's
personal involvement in the Dah Sun Cotton Mill in Nan-
t'ung, viewing him as an exceptional success.

Lin Shan-i ("Chang Chien's Practical Thought,"[a]
Nagoya gakuin daigaku ronshu--shakai kagaku hen 17.1)
deals with Chang Chien by emphasizing that his views on
the encouragement of practical affairs and his focus on
the importance of the cotton and the steel and iron industries coexisted with his Confucian ideas favoring
agriculture. All were combined in a transitional form
that was not fully developed. He and Nakai both address
the issue of Chang's fame as a Hanlin graduate.

In the same issue of Shakai keizai shigaku that
featured Nakai's article there is Takamura Naosuke's
essay, "The Formation of the Japanese Cotton Spinning
Industry in China,"[a] which describes how the Japanese
spinning industry in its formative years prior to World
War I exported capital through commercial firms. Takamura points out that the Mitsui Company, which purchased
spun yarn in Shanghai, implemented a managerial reform
of the managerial agency system and put an end to the
employment of compradors. Together with Nakai's essay,
these two pieces raise important questions about the
transformation of the traditional economic system. But
issues still remain as to the significance of opportuni-

ties [for transformations] in the pre-modern period.

In his essay, "The Establishment of the Commercial
Bank of China and the Hong Kong-Shanghai Bank in 1896:
Sheng Hsüan-huai's Plan"[a] (Hitotsubashi ronsō 84.4),
Hamashita Takeshi discusses the debate over the establishment of the Commercial Bank of China, advocated by
Sheng Hsüan-huai in the "second era of opening the
country" -- from the Sino-Japanese War through the Anglo-
Chinese Commercial Treaty. He points out that "critics
and supporters alike demonstrated both perplexity and
anxiety in the recognition and response to the loans
from foreign banks when they were first introduced."
However, Hamashita's analysis of "the results of the
bank movement itself" awaits the further publication of
his work. I must also note here a major work by
Professor Hamashita: Chūgoku kindai keizai shi kankei
kaidai tsuki bunken mokuroku (Annotated bibliography of
materials relating to the economic history of modern
China).[b]

We also have Takashimo Hiroaki's essay, "The Peiyang
Warlord Regime and Finance Capital"[a] (Shigaku ronsō).
Takashimo claims that the warlords were basically landlord regimes. He analyzes the differences between
finance capital in the Communications Clique and the
Pei-hsi-hsing Clique, the backbone of the Peiyang warlords, and he clarifies the changes in alignments between
them and the warlord governments.

Subjected to international capitalist pressure, in
what way did China's traditional social and economic
structure respond and undergo transformation? First,
for a study from a political perspective, we have Sasaki
Hiroshi, "Westernization and Troop Training"[a] (Nakajima
ronshū, vol. 1). He argues that although the Westerni-
zers took part in comprador, anti-popular activities in
the later period, "in their earlier activities they an-
ticipated [China's] colonization and were anxious about

the need for preserving national sovereignty."

Ōsawa Kazuo, in his essay "Westernizing Officials
and the Sino-French War: The Shanghai China Merchants'
Steam Navigation Company"[a] (Keiō gijuku daigaku gengo
bunka kenkyūjo kiyō 11), clarifies how Li Hung-chang
took advantage of the establishment of the Grain Tribute
Treaty between the China Merchants' Steam Navigation
Company and the Nyugẽñ Dynasty [1802-1945] in Vietnam
and used intelligence from the Company in negotiating
with the French.

There remains a need for further structural studies
of the trends and nature of political power in the late
Ch'ing. One article that analyzes the transformation
of the ruling structure, particularly in rural villages,
from the Westernization period on, is Kojima Yoshio's
"The City and the Village in the Late Ch'ing: The Kiangnan Region"[a] (Shichō N.S. 8). As in his very considerable studies to date, Kojima sees the relationship between city and countryside in the late Ch'ing as one of
opposition between merchants and landlords resident in
the cities, on the one hand, and the local farming populace, on the other. He argues that the political upheavals of the late Ch'ing "unfolded as a resistance
movement by the rural farming population against the increase in feudal exactions by the gentry-landlords resident in the cities or their equals in status, the large
merchants who cooperated closely with the Westernizing
(yang-wu) officials who were the bulwark of Ch'ing
power." We can see in Kojima's framework: (a) the trend
toward the "dissolution of the natural economy" because
of the "economic intrusion of capitalist powers that,
although based in the cities, permeated down to the
rural villages"; and (b) the fact that even as part of
this process the Sheng-tse chen[elites], for example,
"did not deal in cocoons, even though mechanized spinning mills were established in the Kiangnan region

centering around Shanghai, nor did they allow in one
cocoon merchant." Thinking both of this and of the
Suzuki article cited above, can we say that, structurally,
traditional society had the power to resist foreign
pressure while domestically the cities continued to
exploit the countryside?

To make the opposing case, one can see a certain
"spring-like reaction," as it were, often functioning in
the transformative process of late Ch'ing society, and
the phenomenological effect it had on China's "lateness
to modernity." Yet, what role did this spring effect
play? Takahashi Kōsuke's essay, "Land Tax, Rent, and
Local Magistrates: The Case of Kiangnan in the Early
Modern Era"[a] (Tōyōshi kenkyū 39.2) analyzes the substantive processes by which a county magistrate collected
taxes. He points out that we should bear in mind, when
we evaluate the class nature of the county magistrate
as public [i.e., official] authority, that from the
tenants' perspective the magistrate embodied "the reproduction of a fleeting illusion of public authority,"
for the magistrate did not have to respond to tenants'
demands in his capacity as the public authority.[2]
Takahashi's analysis of the change in public authority
accompanying the transformation of the gentry-landlord
stratum after the Taiping Rebellion remains to be done.
It is hoped that future analyses will examine the en-
tirety of the modern period in conjunction with the process of the dissolution of feudal ties in rural villages.

On gentry-landlords immediately after the Taiping
Rebellion, we have Yamana Hirofumi's article, "Charitable Estates in Kiangnan in the Late Ch'ing"[a] (Tōyō
gakuhō 62.1-2). Yamana clarifies the way in which the
restoration of private property and the maintenance of
rent collection (the prerequisites for the reorganization of the landlord system) took place through the expansion of charitable estates based on the traditional

ideal of clan cohesion. Surely problems posed by China's
traditional principles and structures underlay the late
Ch'ing, despite the success or failure of various reforms at that time.

For example, Watanabe Atsushi's "On the Policy to
Centralize Power in the Salt Administration of the Late
Ch'ing"[b] (Nakajima ronshū, vol. 1) examines the reform
of the salt administration, which he sees as one link
in the larger policy of centralizing power carried out
by the late Ch'ing government; and he argues that it was
first brought to fruition in the Republican period.
Ever since the 1898 Reform, there had been a movement
toward the establishment of a modern state with centralized power that counteracted the post-Taiping trend toward "concentration of power in the governor-general."
Watanabe also points out that these policies were unable
to root out the abuses in the salt administration.

Watanabe has also written "The Formation and Development of Modern Japanese Colonial Salt Enterprises (1):
Meiji-Taishō Eras"[c] (Kumamoto daigaku kyōiku gakubu kiyō
29). He sheds light on how the Japanese expansion of
salt enterprises in the Meiji and Taishō periods relied
on the pre-existing production structure of Chinese salt
manufacture techniques as well as on the small producer
system and the boss (pa-t'ou) system. This point hints
at problems shared by salt manufacturing and cotton mills.

In his essay, "The Kung-i hui of Ying-k'ou"[a]
(Rekishigaku kenkyū 481), Kurahashi Masanao analyzes the
Kung-i hui or "merchant guilds" that were formed in
various northeastern cities from the mid-19th into the
20th centuries. He shows that through "a system of
transferable currency" the tradition of Kung-i hui demonstrated a resistance both to warlords in the Republican period and to control of northeastern China by the
Japanese. The result, however, was that "imperialism
did not allow a civic consciousness to mature," a

situation that led to the continuation of "a system out
of step with the times." Yet, the problem remains as to
just what this "civic consciousness" in modern China is.

One essay that sees modern China's political upheavals as "an example of political change in places
that incorporated as peripheral states in the world
capitalist system" and that argues that this phenomenon
must be addressed structurally as well as from the perspective of social history is Yumoto Kunio's "A Structural Investigation of the 1911 Revolution: The Social
Historical Importance of Political Change in China's
Southwest in 1911, the Case of K'un-ming"[a] (Tōyō bunka
kenkyūjo kiyō 81). Yumoto criticizes past research,
based on the methods of social and economic history,
and doubts the picture presented when the terminology
of the "constitutionalists" and the "revolutionaries" is
used. He seeks to find a new handle on the subject,
with the main object of his analysis being the process
of the formation of the New Army in Yunnan. We would
like to see him apply models from the work of Skinner
and Kuhn when dealing with the structural transformation
of village society that was the basis for this political
change, and for him to provide concrete evidence thereof.
Furthermore, the phenomenon of differences in research
methodologies leading to a total fragmentation among
research-[produced] histories that are of necessity based
on those methodologies, is food for thought for all
people who are doing research on the same subject.

Two essays associated with Skinner's model and
dealing with rural markets are Ishida Hiroshi, "Market
and Marriage Areas in Rural China of Old"[b] (Shirin 63.5);
and Hayashi Kazuo, "Hsü and Shih in Kwangtung During the
Ming and Ch'ing: An Investigation of the Forms and
Functions of Traditional Markets"[a] (Shirin 63.1). Ishida
argues that the arena for the daily life of the Chinese
peasantry consisted of "various intermediary structures

related by region and blood, through the village, clan,
or relatives"; these comprised the market area -- a
community for living (seikatsu kyōdōtai). Hayashi
traces the changes in traditional markets in Kwangtung
from the middle of the Ch'ing dynasty onward.

Next, we have Arita Kazuo's essay, "Toward a Theory
of the Structure of Consciousness in the Late Ch'ing"[a]
(Tōkyō gaikokugo daigaku ronshū 30); this article provides an outline of late Ch'ing intellectual history and
is particularly concerned with the intellectual ideas
of individuals and groups engaged in reform. Arita understands the sense of crisis in the late Ch'ing as
something that grew more and more profound by stages.
He points that in the post-Boxer years, in order to
make up for China's "lateness" and "to meet the world
powers as an equal or superior," the arguments for revolution were developed simultaneously in racial and political veins. Furthermore, among those intent on reform
who were of a strong "literati consciousness" and came
from the "middle ranks in society" there was no "conception of trying to systematize the sense of crisis within
the life dimensions of a 'citizenry' to carry out reform
energetically."

Arita does not develop this latter problem in concrete terms. Similarly, Kihara Katsuji, in his essay
"Liang Ch'i-ch'ao's Conception of the Modern State in
the Late Ch'ing"[a] (Ritsumeikan bungaku 418-421), discusses how Liang "advocated statism (kuo-chia-chu-i) and
stressed self-awakening and popular sovereignty for the
undifferentiated masses as citizens of the modern state,"
but he fails to explain the link between Liang's activities and these "undifferentiated masses."

On the other hand, we have Shinozaki Moritoshi's
"A Short Essay on Yang Tu-sheng: The Wanderings and
Death of a Narodnik"[a] (Kumatsu shū 2) which investigates
in great detail the activities of Yang Tu-sheng. Yang

suffered many defeats in the revolutionary movement from
the uprising of the army he personally led until the
1911 Revolution itself. Jolted by his experiences amid
the "Narodniki"[3] and "terrorists," he ended his life in
suicide. Shinozaki raises the issue of the meaning of
Yang's personal frustrations: "He had no choice but to
end his life because of the failure of his personal
raison d'être ([and by extension] that of the 'middle
ranks of society' or the intelligentsia) in the world
of the 20th century."

     Yang Tu-sheng may have to come to destruction, ago-
nizing over whether he as a member of the "middle ranks
of society" could become part of the revolution. By
contrast, Kubota Bunji traces in his essay "Sun Yat-sen's
Land Equalization Policy"[b] (Rekishigaku kenkyū 478) the
formation of Sun's ideas on land equalization, their
development, and their place in the history of [land]
theories; at the same time, he argues, Sun repressed his
own convictions regarding revolutionary theory and popular livelihood that "emerged from his personal knowledge
as the son of an impoverished peasant." Kubota empha-
sizes that Sun consistently advocated a policy of national ownership of the land. Despite the fact that the
idea of land equalization (which had "socialist over-
tones" to it) could only in fact suggest a compromising
and abstract policy, Sun Yat-sen's thought "stuck to a
utopianism transcending the dimension of immediate plans,
policies, and propaganda that were thought realizable in
the near future," and he accepted a radical and progressive vision of the future. Kubota argues that, on the
basis of the slogan "he who tills the land shall possess
it" [land to the tiller], Sun's ideas developed to a
stage that showed the necessity of the firm establishment
of peasant ownership of the land.

     In contrast to this essay is Ikeda Makoto's "Lenin's
Notion of Democratic Revolution in Asia: Lenin on Sun

Yat-sen"[a] (Ritsumeikan hōgaku 149). Ikeda indicates
that in 1924 Sun Yat-sen came to the realization that
"land to the tiller" meant a thorough revolution. Sun
thought that because the people who "were aware of the
national crisis" were landlords and because the peasantry
"was incapable of resisting the landlords," "land to the
tiller" would remain a problem for the future. This
interpretation is rather different in stress from that
of Kubota's essay.

On Sun Yat-sen, we also have Takenaka Hiroaki's
"Notes on Sun Yat-sen's Knowledge of Asia"[b] (Yasuda
gakuen kenkyū kiyō 20). Takenaka argues that Sun's
anti-imperialism and his conception of the liberation
of the oppressed peoples of Asia were supported with
"'a sinocentric notion of relief assistance' for the
'weak minority peoples' living along China's borders."

Matsumoto Hideki's essay, "Sung Chiao-jen and the
Chien-tao Question[4]: Tracing the Patriotic Revolutionary
Movement"[a] (Ritsumeikan bungaku 418-421), is concerned
with how the revolutionaries groped with making China
a "strong nation" during the period of the 1911 Revolution. He analyzes in detail Sung Chiao-jen's concern
over the Chien-tao issue together with the maneuverings
of Uchida Ryōhei and the Isshinkai over Chien-tao. He
describes Sung as having the character of a "politician"
and sees his "patriotic" activities in later years as
one element of Sung's notion of how a central revolution
could bring about a "political situation which would
hasten the establishment of a parliamentary government
without compromising with Yüan Shih-k'ai."

The period just after the 1911 Revolution had
produced little research, but one essay that looks at the
Assembly of the Republic of China is Hazama Naoki's
"The Victory of the Kuomintang in the Elections to the
First National Assembly of the Republic of China"[c] (Tōhō
gakuhō 52). Hazama stresses that the framework of the

political history of the early Republic, which unfolded
in the opposition of the Assembly and the Peiyang warlords, "grew out of the victory of the Kuomintang in the
first Assembly elections and that this victory was one
result of the 'success' of the 1911 Revolution." He argues that the victory shows "that in semi-feudal China
to achieve victory in a movement with any mass base
necessitated consistently raising the banner of anti-
imperialism and anti-feudalism." Yet, a question remains as to how we are to connect and understand this
"banner of anti-imperialism and anti-feudalism" with
the content of Huang Hsing's speech in Hunan for the
defense of the principle of people's livelihood, a
speech listened to by many people in an audience that
included landlords "who scarcely understood the essence
of the matter under discussion."

In his essay, "On the Formation of the Constitutionalist Party in Hunan"[a] (Nagoya daigaku Tōyōshi kenkyū
hōkoku 6), Shimizu Minoru discusses the "political and
economic processes through which" the constitutionalists
"emerged and coalesced" in the 1911 period. How are we,
however, to combine the opposition to Ch'ing rule in the
name of the people that is pointed out here with the
crisis in the local gentry control structure caused by
the rise of popular unrest?

We also have Nakayashiki Hiroshi's article "The New
Culture Movement of May Fourth and Ch'en Tu-hsiu: A Study
of the Intellectual Foundations of Modern Chinese Literature"[a] (Bunkei ronsō 15.1). He discusses the process by
which enlightenment thinkers who were captivated by
modern Western thought came to be hostile to the popular
anti-imperialist struggle.

The various incidents that have served as topics
for the above essays indicate aspects of "modernity" in
China, but, as we noted at the beginning, we are also
witnessing at present a continuous exposure by China of

her own "backwardness." Although there are people who
ignore the Japanese imperialist invasion in modern
Chinese history and advocate a new "theory of stagnation,"[5] there is a need to readdress Japan's past understanding of China. Published work from various fields
concerning modern Sino-Japanese relations include the
following: Kageyama Masahiro, "On the Education of
Overseas Chinese Students at the Kōbun gakuin in the
Late Ch'ing"[a] (Kumatsu shū 2), which introduces historical sources unearthed in the Kōdōkan library; Hosono
Kōji, "The Idea of 'Protecting China' and the 'Koreani-
zation' of China: Ōkuma Shigenobu's View of the Outside
World and One of Its Consequences"[b] (Shikan 102); Nozawa
Yutaka, "The Russo-Japanese War and East Asia, with Em-
phasis on the Question of Manchuria and Mongolia"[c]
(Shichō N.S. 7); Yamaguchi Osamu, "The Establishment of
a Postal Accord Between Japan and China (I)"[a] (Seishin
joshi daigaku ronsō 55); Baba Akira, "The Issue of the
Full Cancellation of Indemnities for the North China
Incident [Boxers]"[a] (Kokugakuin daigaku kiyō 18).

Among these essays we also find Hara Motoko's and
Komatsubara Tomoko's "An Elucidation of the Indistinct
in the Research of Wang Kuo-wei"[a] (Kumatsu shū 2). They
translate two essays from Wang's Li-shih yen-chiu
(Historical studies): "Yin-Chou chih-tu lun" (The institutions of the Shang and Chou): and "Ta-tan lun" (A
study of the Tartars). In their "elucidation of the
indistinct," the authors address various questions relating to Wang. Hara has also written "Ajia" no koro:
Seikyōsha ni okeru Naitō Konan o chūshin ni (The Ajia
era: Naitō Konan's years in the Seikyōsha)[a] in which
she examines the state of knowledge about China among
modern Japanese scholars of East Asia. The former essay
doubts the commonly held theories surrounding both the
meaning of Wang Kuo-wei's Li-shih yen-chiu and the reason for his suicide. They try to portray with corrob-

orative evidence Wang's accumulating distress caused
by such things as the chaos in China after the collapse
of the Ch'ing, his contacts with Japanese scholars, and
the Japanese advance into China.

Nomura Kōichi, in his essay "Tachibana Shiraki: A
Variation on Pan-Asianism"[a] (Rikkyō hōgaku 19), examines
the understanding of China demonstrated in a specific
Japanese person's concerns over China. Nomura dubs
Tachibana the "last runner"[6] for Pan-Asianism.

Many essays were unavoidably excluded in our introduction to the above articles on the substantive state
of affairs in "modern times." Among those others dealing with concrete issues in rural society, we have:
Nakamura Jihee, "Various Questions Concerning Villages
in Hopei in the Early Republic: A Written Report on Wu-
ch'ing County near the Capital"[a] (Chūō daigaku bungakubu
kiyō-shigakka 25); Ōtani Toshio, "Water Conservancy
Customs in Kiangnan in the Ch'ing Dynasty and the Hsiang-
tung System"[c] (Shirin 63.1); Morita Akira, "Well-Water
Irrigation in North China and the Development of Well-
Digging Projects: Hopei in the Early Republic"[c] (in
Shigaku ronsō); Morita Akira, "An Issue Concerning Water
Utilization on Polder Lands under the Republic: The
Introduction of Irrigation and Drainage Facilities"[d]
(Ajia keizai 21.1); Yamada Keiko, "Notes on General Conditions in North Chinese Villages in the First Half of
the Twentieth Century"[a] (Hiroshima daigaku Tōyōshi
kenkyūshitsu hōkoku 2); and Noguchi Tetsurō, "The Chen-
k'ung Sect and the Wu-wei Sect; or the Liao-tsu ching
and the Lo-tsu ching"[c] (Rekishi jinrui 9).

In the area of foreign relations, Obata Tatsuo's
article "The Conclusion of the Wang-hsia Treaty: An
Introduction to the History of Early Sino-American Negotiations (2)"[a] (Ritsumeikan bungaku 418-421) deals with
Sino-American relations. Also, there is Sasaki Masaya's
essay "A Study of the Opium War"[a] (Kindai Chūgoku 7, 8)

which is still unfinished.

Three essays deal with Japanese activities in
Taiwan: Nakamura Takashi, "The Tō-A shoin and the Tōbun
gakudō: The Origin of Educational Facilities in South
China under the [Japanese] Governor-General of Taiwan"[a]
(Tenri daigaku gakuhō 31.4); Nakamura Takashi, "The Tōei
gakudō in Foochow and the Kyokuhei gakudō in Amoy: The
Beginning of Educational Facilities in South China under
the Office of the [Japanese] Governor-General of Taiwan"[b]
(Tenri daigaku gakuhō 32.2); and Itō Teruo, "The Taiwan
Cultural Association and the Taiwan People's Party: The
Significance of Their Confrontation"[b] (Yokohama shiritsu
daigaku ronsō--Jimbun kagaku keiritsu 31.2-3).

Included in the volume Kindai Nihon to Higashi Ajia
(Modern Japan and East Asia) are a number of articles
which concern issues in modern East Asian history. The
volume itself deserves a book review.

On Ch'ing financial administration, we have two
essays: Ichiko Shōzō, "A Study of the History of Currency in the Ch'ing"[a] (Takushoku daigaku ronshū 127, 129,
130); and Kataoka Kazutada, "A Study of the Likin Bureaus
in Yunnan During the Reign of the Kuang-hsü Emperor"[b]
(Nakajima ronshū, vol. 2). Kasahara Tokuji's article
"Chaos in the Peking Financial Administration During the
Period of the May Fourth Movement"[a] (Utsunomiya daigaku
kyōiku gakubu kiyō 30.1) deals with the period of the
Peiyang warlords.

In the field of intellectual history, we have
Maruyama Matsuyuki's essay "Notes on Materials for a
Biography of Li Ta-chao (1)"[a] (Tōkyō daigaku kyōyō
gakubu jimbun kagakka kiyō 71). Also, Enoki Kazuo's
essay "Tung Hsün and His Writings, Especially His Diary"[a]
(Kindai Chūgoku 7, 8) is being published serially like
Sasaki Masaya's piece cited above.

Looking over the articles that I have introduced
thus far, it seems that there were few essays in the

field of the history of popular rebellions. Two essays
dealt with trends in Chinese research [in this field]
in a comprehensive way: Matsuzaki Tsuneko, "Studies of
the History of Peasant Wars in Contemporary China, with
a Focus on the Post-Mao Period"[a] (Sundai shigaku 50);
and Sōda Saburō, "Recent Chinese Studies on the History
of Peasant Wars"[b] (Ajia kenkyū, Hiroshima University 2).
Kobayashi Kazumi has written two essays on the White
Lotus Rebellion of the Ch'ing: "The Ti-wang and the
Sheng-mu in the White Lotus Rebellion in China: The
Dualistic World of a Pseudo-Community"[b] (Rekishigaku no
saiken ni mukete 5); and "The Character of the White
Lotus Rebellion of the Chia-ch'ing"[a] (Nakajima ronshū,
vol. 1).

Only two essays, however, dealt with modern rebellions: Harigaya Miwako, "Local Rule in the Later Period
of the Taiping Rebellion: Chekiang from 1860 on"[a]
(Hitotsubashi ronsō 83.5); and Namiki Yorihisa, "Chang
Lo-hsing, Leader of the Nien Army"[b] (Kumatsu shū 2).
Harigaya points out that the "contradictions in the
policies of the Taipings, who opted for a system of local
officials whose first priority was the procurement
of military provisions." She argues that this system
served the landlords and local gentry as a "mediating
structure" for preserving past local village control
under Taiping occupation. Although she places low-level
functionaries and vagrants who held a large number of
local offices in the same category with landlords and
local gentry, I feel that this view does not appear in
the language used in the historical materials. My own
essay tries to assess the historical nature of the Nien
Army through its leader Chang Lo-hsing, but I did not
clarify the internal structure of peasant uprisings in
the Huai-pei area.

MING-CH'ING STUDIES IN JAPAN: 1981

Asai Motoi, in
Shigaku zasshi 91.5
(May 1982), 212-19.

The Gentry

An understanding of the composition and the historical roles played by the strata known as hsiang-shen, shen-chin, and shen-shih [all translated as "gentry" in English] in the political, economic, and cultural arenas during the Ming-Ch'ing period has become one of our central topics for research in recent years. A large number of studies published last year dealt with this issue. The main direction of these essays has been the attempt to stipulate more strictly on an empirical basis the concepts of hsiang-shen, shen-chin, and shen-shih that have thus far been used differently by scholars, and to build the foundation for future research.

Yamane Yukio's work is representative of this trend. In his two articles cited below, Yamane limits the use of the term hsiang-shen to retired officials of the seventh grade or higher and those who passed the chin-shih degree and were residing in their native area. He refers to retired officials below the seventh grade -- chü-jen, kung-sheng, sheng-yüan, and chien-sheng -- all as shih. The term he uses to designate both groups collectively is, appropriately, shen-shih. He points out in particular the need to pay attention to the differences between shen (or hsiang-shen) and shih.

One essay that analyzes the shih class from institutional as well as practical aspects is Oh Keum-sung's "On the Formative Process of the Shen-shih Class in the

Ming Period"[b] (Mindaishi kenkyū 9, translated [from the
Korean] by Yamane Yukio and Inada Hideko). This latter
half of a two-part essay[1] discusses the sheng-yüan and
chien-sheng from the mid-Ming on. The number of sheng-
yüan gradually grew from about 30,000 in the early Ming
to over 500,000 by the late Ming. As a consequence, the
great majority of them had scarcely any possibility of
rising to a bureaucratic post. Similarly, in the early
Ming chien-sheng had a chance of receiving a position,
but with the mid-15th century enactment of regulations
on chien-sheng, their number increased tremendously until it was virtually impossible to gain office with
chien-sheng status alone. From the mid-Ming on, shih
(men with chü-jen, sheng-yüan, and chien-sheng degrees
who had not yet assumed a post) began to form a more
identifiable group distinct from shen. At the same time,
the two groups formed a unit, shen-shih, clearly distinct
from the general populace, and they expressed themselves
in the political and social arenas.

In this connection, Wada Masahiro has written "A
Study of the Use of the Expression Hsiang-shen in the
Late Ming and Early Ch'ing"[f] (Kyūshū daigaku Tōyōshi
ronshū 9). Wada analyzes the concepts of hsiang and
shen in the expression hsiang-shen. He argues that
hsiang was used in the sense of "local village" or "same
origin" in reference to the regional divisions of province, prefecture, department, and county. Shen referred
in a narrow sense to those who had held bureaucratic
office, and in a wider sense it came to include chü-jen
in the Ch'ung-chen reign at the end of the Ming, kung-
sheng and chien-sheng in early Ch'ing, and sheng-yüan
in the late Ch'ing.

Wada has also written "A Study of Shen-shih Status
from the Late Ming and Early Ch'ing Onward"[g] (Mindaishi
kenkyū 9). He argues that from the latter half of the
Ming the expression shen-shih (which had always indicated

an official in office) began to appear with shen and
shih having distinct meanings; in the Ch'ing shen and
shih (or shen and chin) became official, legal terms,
and shih indicated sheng-yüan (or kung-sheng, chien-
sheng, and sheng-yüan). On the other hand, in the area
of local politics, from the latter half of the Ch'ing,
shih seemed to be undergoing a transformation toward
shen. One cause for this change was the favorable legal
treatment, consolidated in the Yung-cheng and Ch'ien-
lung reigns, which protected the honor as well as the
actual benefits gained by the special privileges of
shih. As in his other essay, Wada argues that this indicates the rise of shih toward shen.

In connection with Wada's work, Yamane has already
pointed out that it is unnecessary to consider hsiang
as related to the administrative unit of the same name.
One problem that remains is that if he [Wada] claims
that shih rose to shen status, then how does he explain
the phenomenon of class formation from the late Ming into the Ch'ing through the growing distinction between
shen and shih and the decrease in the possibilities for
shih to be upwardly mobile? In addition to these basic
studies of shen-shih status, we have the following articles which analyze the actual make-up and roles of the
gentry.

Fuma Susumu's article, "A Supplementary Analysis of
[my article] 'Riots of Scholars Against Local Officials
in the Late Ming'"[b] (Toyama daigaku jimbun gakubu kiyō
4), introduces two historical sources held in the Peking
Library in his discussion of riots by shih at the end of
the Ming. There existed locally at that time "gentry
assemblies" (kung-i)[2] made up of hsiang-shen, chü-jen,
and sheng-yüan; and from time to time they led movements
against local officials. Fuma argues that these "assemblies" were opened to the general public as well. The
problem is what happened to them in the Ch'ing.

Matsuda Yoshirō's essay, "The Opening of Sand Flats
in the Pearl River Delta in Kwangtung and the Emergence
of Gentry Control in the Late Ming and Early Ch'ing"[a]
(Shakai keizai shigaku 46.6), discusses how the hsiang-
shen in the Pearl River delta effected control over a
wide range of local products and formed a ruling structure by using clan cohesiveness in the opening of sand
flats during the late Ming and early Ch'ing years.

In his essay, "Hsü Ch'ien-hsüeh and His Two Brothers:
A Concrete Case of Local Control by Kiangnan Gentry"[e]
(Tōyōshi kenkyū 40.3), Kawakatsu Mamoru reexamines an
issue he has already studied. He uses archival sources
recently published by the Chinese to look at the miscon-
duct at the local level in the early Ch'ing of the great
Hsü gentry (hsiang-shen) family from K'un-shan county,
Soochow prefecture. Kawakatsu offers us an important
case study of how the hsiang-shen lived by showing how
the Hsü family came to dominate local society by having
built up a power structure with their clansmen, in-laws,
bondservants (nu-p'u), ruffians, retainers, local officials, clerks and runners, and yamen underlings.

Yamane Yukio's article, "The Composition of the
Gentry [Shen-shih] Class in Shang-ch'eng, Honan"[c]
(Tōyōshi kenkyū 40.2), analyzes the ratios and residential distribution of the various groups within the gentry
(hsiang-shen, chü-jen, chien-sheng, and sheng-yüan) from
Shang-ch'eng county, based on the list of the names of
gentry who contributed to the publication of Shang-ch'eng
hsien-chih in the Chia-ch'ing reign. He points out that
while upper level gentry lived comparatively close to
the county seat, lower level gentry were scattered over
the entire county. Future research on hsiang-shen and
shen-shih needs to address the nature and composition of
the various elements that made up these groups and to
clarify the historical conditions by which they became
social classes with names such as shen-shih and shen-chin.

Popular Rebellions

A number of essays in the field of popular rebellions were concerned with shen and shih. Taniguchi Kikuo's "A Study of Peasant Rebellions in the Late Ming"[c] (Ōsaka daigaku kyōyōbu kenkyū shūroku-Jimbun shakai kagaku 28) notes that we have yet to come up with a theory that provides a unified explanation of the two forms of rebellion in the late Ming: (a) rent resistance and bondservant uprisings primarily in South and Central China; and (b) roving bandits in North China. He also argues that officials and local gentry (hsiang-shen) in North China, such as Lü K'un, in order to surmount the crisis affecting their control over rural villages, tried to institute reforms (consistent with those in the Kiangnan delta) in order to do such things as limit the privilege of corvée exemption (yu-mien) for hsiang-shen and to equalize corvée burdens. He notes that these reforms did not touch the basic problem of land, added to the low level of productivity and the strengthening of state exactions, and were out of touch with reality. In the final analysis, they invited popular rebellions against gentry control. Furthermore, he points out the need to explain the link between local bandits and peasant groups, and mentions this with respect to the internal structure of Li Tzu-ch'eng's army.

In his essay, "Peasant Rebellions and the Gentry Response at the End of the Ming"[d] (in Nakajima ronshū, vol. 2), Yamane Yukio points out that a clear class differentiation developed in the late Ming between the upper gentry or hsiang-shen and the lower gentry centered around the sheng-yüan. In order to take advantage of opportunities to rise from their oppressed position, the lower gentry occasionally participated in peasant uprisings. Yamane argues that they did not do this out of a sense of solidarity with the peasantry and that their basic nature [as an elite] remained unchanged.

Satō Fumitoshi, in his essay "A Study of the Ta-shun
Local Government: The Case of the 'Hsiang-ching' Regime"[a3]
(in Nakajima ronshū, vol. 2) notes that the "Hsiang-ching"
regime, the basis of Li Tzu-ch'eng's power, took shape
by employing local officials, hsiang-shen, and sheng-yüan
as civil officials in Honan and Hupeh in the late Ming;
local and roving bandits, Ming generals, and bondservants were also turned into military officials. He
shows how the hsiang-shen, sheng-yüan, and big landowners
in this area constructed a large number of fortresses
and came to resist the "Hsiang-ching" regime.

In his article, "Bandits' Spies in the Late Ming"[a]
(Nagoya daigaku Tōyōshi kenkyū hōkoku 7), Yoshio Hiroshi
analyzes the military tactics of bandits prior to the
appearance of Li Tzu-ch'eng. He argues that their offen-
sive strategy was based on linking the main body of rebel
troops with spies. Among the spies were residents of the
areas into which rebels had advanced; and the spies fur-
tively watched the government's troop movements, engaged
in secret dealings within the cities, and bought necessary provisions.

One essay that discusses vagabonds (wu-lai) as
leaders of peasant rebellions is Ueda Makoto, "Social
Relations of Vagabonds in the Cities of Kiangnan in the
Late Ming and Early Ch'ing: Thugs (ta-hang) and Porters
(chiao-fu)"[a] (Shigaku zasshi 90.11). According to Ueda,
although there was a disintegration of peasant groupings
and an emergence of vagabonds through the mid-Ming, in
most cases they were apprehended and brought under landlord control. At the end of the Ming, however, the
growth of commercial economy resulted in locally powerful men residing in the county capitals. As a result,
the stage was set for vagabond activities. Thugs and
porters who were urban vagabonds dealt in violence, were
organized and had their own spheres of influence, and
received the protection of hsiang-shen and the local men

of influence. They became active in the Wan-li reign
toward the end of the Ming and reached their zenith in
the Ch'ung-chen era. In the Ch'ing, he argues, the
thugs declined and the porters were brought under control through the intrusion of state power. How the
vagabonds lived under Ch'ing control remains for future
research to explore.

Kawakatsu Mamoru's essay, "Pettifoggers in the Late
Ming and Early Ch'ing: A Kind of Lumpen-Intelligentsia
in Old China"[f] (Tōyōshi ronshū 9), investigates lumpen-
intellectual pettifoggers who acted as attorneys, con-
tractors, and conflict-resolvers in court cases. With
the decline of the li-chia system that accompanied the
disappearance of the li-lao-jen system, these men took
on tasks formerly handled by li-lao-jen: small matters
among the people, buying and selling agricultural produce, and lawsuits arising out of quarrels or murder.

Morality books, a medium by which local gentry-
landlords exercised their educative authority, constituted one intellectual effort to maintain the feudal
order, according to Okuzaki Yūji, "The Lifestyle of the
People of the Lower Classes in the Ming"[b] (Senshū shigaku
13). These books enjoined the li-chang[4] and the chia-
shou[5] to protect life and preserve the social order
through [promoting] mutual trust, and to carry out
properly the population survey for the household registers. Okuzaki also notes that these books were critical
of the local gentry to the extent that they counselled
landlords to be compassionate toward tenant farmers and
masters to deal magnanimously with their servants. Yet,
on the other hand, there were those among the lower
classes, he argues, who used the ideas expressed in the
morality books to criticize the way the local gentry lived.

Suzuki Chūsei's essay, "The Anti-Ch'ing Movement of
Ma Ch'ao-chu in 1752: A Utopian Movement Among the Chinese
People"[b] (in Ichiko ronshū) concerns the Ma Ch'ao-chu

case of 1752. Ma's religious sect believed in a charis-
matic person [Ma] who could perform miracles and magic,
and they believed in the magic he performed. Their
clearly political slogan, "Down with the Ch'ing, revive
the Ming," Suzuki argues, became intertwined with pre-
dictions of the coming of cataclysm and of a prosperous
world blessed with great wealth in gold and silver,
which gave the movement its millenarian ideology. Ma's
followers were merchants and reclaimers of mountain
lands in the provinces of Hupeh, Anhwei, and Honan.

     Another work in the category of popular rebellions
is Mori Masao's "Bondservant Uprisings and Rent Resistance, Late Ming and Early Ch'ing: Popular Resistance
Movements in Local Society in Central and South China"[i]
(in the report on research results of the 1979-80 sub-
sidy for scientific research, general research, part C:
Kōsō undō no chōkiteki hikakuteki sōgōteki kenkyū (Long-
term, comparative, and synthetic research on rent resistance movements). We hope this work will be separately
reviewed for we shall not deal with it here.

Taxation Systems

     Kuroki Kuniyasu's "The Character of the Labor Ser-
vice Tax (ting-yin) Levy Under the Single Whip System"[a]
(in Nakajima ronshū, vol. 2) argues that in the early
period of the single whip system the labor service tax
was assessed without regard to whether one owned land,
but as the system developed there was a decrease in the
relative weight of the labor service obligation and an
increase in the relative weight given to land ownership.
One sees a fixing of the amounts of labor service and
an end to population censuses. At this stage the single
whip system was basically a mode of control that included
all constituent households under the li-chia system, in
complete contrast to the Yellow Register (huang-ts'e)
system. Without saying that this control was of a

thoroughly personalistic sort as Shigeta Atsushi has
noted, he argues that we should understand this as essentially similar to a land-and-head tax (ti-ting-yin).
However, even though the number of male units (ting) under the single whip system did not reflect the actual
population but remained a fixed number, we must keep in
mind that adult males remained objects of corvée assessment and that, if observed from within the entire structure of the tax system, the li-chia corvée structure and
the organization of local villages continued to exist
after the implementation of the single whip system. Furthermore, the single whip stage was entirely different
in nature from the li-chia stage. I have my doubts if
we can consider it in essence a land-and-head tax system.

Hamashima Atsutoshi has written "The Equitable Field-
Equitable Labor Service System and the Gentry in the Late
Ming and Early Ch'ing (3): Lu Shu-sheng's 'Response to
Kan Tzu-t'ing's Court'"[e] (Shihō 13). He analyzes the
written opposition to the equitable field-equitable labor
service policy that Lu Shu-sheng, a wealthy member of the
gentry from Hua-t'ing county, Sung-chiang prefecture in
the late Ming, communicated to Kan Tzu-chieh [Tzu-t'ing],
the regional inspector from Soochow. Hamashima discusses
the nature of kuan-t'u[6] and kuan-chia[7] systems that were
implemented in Nan-Chih-li and Chekiang in the late Ming,
and he disagrees with Kawakatsu Mamoru's explanation.

Yamamoto Eiji has written on this topic in his "The
Development from the Equitable Field-Equitable Labor Service Policy to the Shun-chuang-fa: The Cases of Wu-chiang
and Chen-tse Counties in the Early Ch'ing"[c] (Yamaguchi
daigaku bungakkaishi 32). Looking at the counties of
Wu-chiang and Chen-tse (Soochow prefecture) in the early
Ch'ing, he investigates the reforms in the taxation system and the local village organization: from the chün-
t'ien chün-i system to the pan-t'u system,[8] to the shun-
chuang system,[9] to a [combined] pan-t'u shun-chuang

system. Yamamoto does not agree that the pan-t'u system,
which was implemented after chün-t'ien chün-i, was based
on fictional divisions created in the villages by chün-
t'ien chün-i or that pan-t'u of the pan-t'u shun-chuang
system was based on the natural villages of the shun-
chuang system. But, exactly what is the basis for
Yamamoto's disagreement?

In his essay, "Another Study of Land Statistics
Relating to the Yü-lin t'u-ts'e (Fish-scale registers)[10]
of Ch'ang-chou County, Soochow Prefecture, in the 1676
Land Survey"[b] (in Nakajima ronshū, vol. 2), Tsurumi
Naohiro provides an analytic investigation that compares:
(a) the fish-scale registers of twenty-four tu[11] and twen-
ty t'u[12] in Ch'ang-chou county, which were prepared for
the 1676 land survey, with (b) the fish-scale registers
of twenty-one tu and eight t'u in the same county that
Tsurumi studied in an earlier essay. He looks at (a)
from the perspectives of land classifications, amounts
of acreage equal to one ch'iu and the various forms of
landholdings (from tax-collecting landlords down to owner-
farmers). In conclusion, he argues: (1) that the amount
of level land equal to one ch'iu in (a) was much less
than in (b), and that each ch'iu of land was divided
again and again ever more narrowly by the households
working on the same ch'iu; and (2) that the number of
owner-farmers and the amount of land they held were
smaller in (a) than in (b). He notes that owner-farmers
were extremely few in number, only about 5% in (a). The
form that landlord-tenant relations took in Tsurumi's
case appears at least to reflect a decline of the peasantry's position. This study offers an important concrete
case of land ownership conditions in the Kiangnan delta
region in the early Ch'ing.

Morita Akira, in his essay "A Reinvestigation of
I-t'u in the Ch'ing Dynasty"[e] (Tōyō gakuhō 62.3-4), continues his work of 1976. Here he discusses the system

of i-t'u (made up of middle and small landowning peasants)
in various locales in Kiangsi and northern Kiangsu that
were characterized by inferior agricultural productivity
and an excessive tax burden. The i-t'u was an autonomous tax-paying organization of individual tax-collecting
households (liang-hu)[13] around the unit of the t'u (i.e.,
the village). In principle, it was divided into ten chia
with a chia-cheng or headman for each chia and a t'u-
chang or village headman. It was run on the basis of
t'u regulations. Although aimed at providing compensa-
tion for the responsibility of tax collection through
the li-chia system (ts'ui-pan),[14] the confusion in
[proper] corvée levies, and tax evasion through proxy
collection, the i-t'u were a mere shell after the Taiping
Rebellion. Because non-payment of taxes increased at
this time, the system was reconstituted with gentry cooperation under official auspices and, changing its basic
nature, was transformed into a proxy tax collection organization centered around the powerful gentry. This
study offers a more empirical and more persuasive response
to Yamamoto Eiji's critique of Morita's earlier work.[15]
Yet, he still has not clarified the nature of those who
he argues played leadership roles in the creation and
operation of i-t'u: namely, hsiang-hsien, ti-fang shih-
shen, and ti-fang kung-cheng shen-ch'i.

Social and Economic History (Other)

The debate of the past few years between Fujii
Hiroshi and Kusano Yasushi over the "One-Field Two-Owners"
system continues. In his essay, "The Deterioration of
Surface Rights in the Late Ming and Early Ch'ing: The
Borders of Ch'ang-chou Prefecture"[g] (Kumamoto daigaku
bungakubu ronsō-Shigaku hen 5), Kusano argues that
"customary topsoil practices (for land on which tenant
labor was invested) developed in the Sung and Yüan and
underwent a substantial transformation in the epochal
Ming-Ch'ing transition." Based on a view he has held

for some time, Kusano adds now that in the late Ming and
early Ch'ing the one-field two-owners system changed into a relationship of bonded rent (ya-tsu).[16] At that
time, in order to compensate for tax losses due to customary topsoil practices along the borders of Ch'ang-chou
prefecture in Fukien, a policy of combining tax payment
in money with produce was implemented and the "double
sale of property" (i-ch'an liang-chia)[17] disappeared.
Furthermore, ownership relations on leased lands (tsu-
t'ien) clearly passed through a transitional period
from K'ang-hsi to Ch'ien-lung.

Critical of Kusano's thesis is Fujii Hiroshi, "The
Basic Structure of the One-Field Two-Owners System (5)"[a]
(Kindai Chūgoku 9). He argues that in the latter part
of the Ming (the Chia-ching era), topsoil rights (in the
larger sense) were established, with a statue of limitations appended, primarily around the issue of bond money
and that in the early Ch'ing there appeared for the first
time what seem to be historical materials on topsoil
rights originating from the labor invested by the tenants.
Fujii claims the notion that perpetual tenancy rights
arose in the Sung and Yüan, as argued by two Chinese
historians -- Han Huan-yü and Liu Yung-ch'eng -- is
erroneous. He also analyzes the value of the new historical materials used by these two scholars, which indicate the existence of rights of perpetual tenancy originating in invested tenant labor in the early Ch'ing.

In Part 6 of his essay (Kindai Chūgoku 10), Fujii
assesses his debate thus far with Kusano. On the two
issues of the "value assigned in the transfer of tenancy
rights" (li-chia chiao-t'ien) and the "buying and selling
of tenancy rights" (tzu-p'ei)[18] evidenced partially on
government lands in the Sung, he criticizes Kusano's
identification of this "value" with the monetary value
of the invested tenant labor. Fujii attacks Kusano for
arguing that this "value" was the current worth of the

land, and that the "repayment money" (so-ch'ou ch'ien or
kuo-chung chih ch'ien, as cited in the story "Shih-yüan
chieh-yin" from the Ch'uo-keng lu) was the monetary value
of the tenant's invested labor. Fujii claims rather that
it was bond money (ya-ch'ien). Furthermore, he assails
Kusano's view that a change toward bonded rent relations
in the one-field two-owners system occurred in the late
Ming and early Ch'ing period. He argues that topsoil
rights gained through labor invested by the tenant changed
to topsoil rights through bonded rent because of the sale
[of the land] and that money for labor investment changed
to bond money because of the resale of tenant farm lands.
Thus, he feels that there could not have been a complete
transition from land obtained through the investment of
tenant labor to land through bonded rent.

Adachi Keiji, in his article "Agricultural Management
and Social Structure in North China in the Ch'ing"[c]
(Shirin 64.4), is critical of the past tendency in Ming-
Ch'ing social and economic historical research to study
the landlord-tenant system of the lower Yangtze delta
region, to see landlord-tenant relations as antagonistic,
and to move from there to a generalization about landlord-
tenant relations for the whole of China. He describes
the agricultural structure of North China, which was
different from Central China. Adachi's analysis of
various agricultural handbooks from North China reveals
the following type of management. It was relatively
large-scale because of two techniques: (a) deep tillage
by increasing the magnitude of animal-drawn ploughs; and
(b) the improvement of soil fertility by using manure
from the livestock to fertilize the soil and by improving
seed strains through selectivity. This type of management, he argues, shaped the life-style of the North
China "gentry." According to Adachi, a minority of the
villages of North China were characterized by large-scale
management and, at the other extreme, a majority by small-

scale ownership or management-supplied laborers for the
large-scale enterprises. He sees this large-scale management beginning to dissipate in the face of the new system of intensified technology that accompanied the emergence of commercial agriculture in the Ch'ing. The
basic research that establishes Adachi's theories of
agricultural technology and management is fundamentally
critical for Ming-Ch'ing social and economic history
that has thus far concentrated on landlord-tenant relations in Kiangnan.

In his essay, "On the Systems of Official-Supplied
and Merchant-Supplied Copper in the Early Ch'ing"[a]
(Tōhoku gakuin daigaku ronshū-Rekishigaku chirigaku 11),
Kōsaka Masanori analyzes these two systems that supported
the work of those in charge of providing copper[19] for
minting in the Shun-chih and K'ang-hsi reigns. He argues
that there was a difference between the value of copper
set by the Board of Revenue and the value given it by
middlemen [on the open market], and that the centrally
appointed officials sent to collect taxes who were responsible for providing copper had to guarantee [the
Board the equivalent of] a large quantity of overvalued
silver taels. In the system of merchant-supplied copper
that replaced the official-supplied system, an excessive
burden similar to this overvalued silver was placed on
the merchant in charge of providing the types of copper.
Furthermore, these designated merchants had perforce to
deliver a substantial amount of "economy" [chieh-sheng,
i.e., silver to reduce expenses] to the imperial household. Yet, he argues, they wanted to comply in order
to secure and strengthen their positions as privileged
merchants. Kōsaka illustrates through this example one
case of official-merchants (kuan-shang) in the Ch'ing.

Water Conservancy
The following three essays appeared in the volume
Satō ronshū. Kawakatsu Mamoru's article "Water Conser-

vancy and the Development of Market Towns in the Yangtze
Delta,"[g] traces the growth of market towns in localities
of the Yangtze delta from the Sung through the Ming
dynasties. He clarifies the links between market towns
and commercial waterways.

Hamashima Atsutoshi's essay, "Background to the
Rise of Yao Wen-hao: A Study of the Chuang-ch'ü i-shu,
by Wei Chiao,"[f] analyzes the background of the emergence
of Yao Wen-hao, who formalized the organization of water
conservancy corvée labor through the li-chia system and
the assessment of labor power by the t'ien-t'ou system.
He attributes Yao's rise to the Wei family of K'un-shan
county [Kiangsu], who rose from local "tax collectors"
(liang-chang)[20] to become an upper gentry family. Hamashima
also notes that the notion of assessing labor service
according to the chao-t'ien[21] method of cultivating wetlands was taking shape among the officialdom before the
early 17th century.

Matsuda Yoshirō's essay, "Water Conservancy Works
in Yin County, Chekiang, in the Ming-Ch'ing Period,"[b]
traces the historical changes from the T'ang through
the Ch'ing in the relations between the state, the local
gentry, and water conservancy usufruct households. He
looks at renovation work and the daily management of
various installations for agricultural and urban water
conservancy in Yin county. He notes in conclusion that:
(a) the actors responsible for the repair and operation
of waterworks changed from officials to water conservancy
usufruct houses to the local gentry; and (b) from the
late Ming, the local gentry controlled water usufruct
households, and they obtained this power over water conservancy from the state. Both Hamashima's and Matsuda's
articles discuss water conservancy in terms of its
close relationship to the local gentry.

Military Institutions

Several authors have dealt with themes concerning

military institutions. Kawagoe Yasuhiro's two-part essay
"A Study of the Alternate Frontier Duty of the Pan-chün[22]
System in the Ming"[b] (Gunji shigaku 16.4 and Shisei 11)
undertakes ground-breaking research to clarify the
pan-chün fan-jung system in which the pan-chün of the
wei-so system, the basis of the Ming military structure,
patrolled the borders with responsibility for the defense
of frontier installations. In Part 1 of his essay,
Kawagoe analyzes troop distibution at various places
within this system. He demonstrates that the great
majority of troops were placed in Pei-Chih-li, Shantung,
Shansi, Honan, Shensi, and Nan-Chih-li. In Part 2, he
describes the composition of the border defense armies
by looking at the garrisons at Pao-ting, Ch'ang-p'ing,
Hsüan-fu, Chi, Shansi, Ta-t'ung, Ninghsia, Yü-lin, Kansu,
and elsewhere. We look forward to further work in this
area.

    Ishibashi Takao has written "The Formation of the
Bayara in the Early Ch'ing: The T'ien-ming Period [1616-
1626]"[a] (Chūgoku kindaishi kenkyū 1). In it he analyzes
the Bayara military system during the period of Nurhaci's
rule, and he describes how in 1623, due to the social
upheavals caused by Nurhaci's invasion of Liaotung, there
was a reorganization of the Bayara system that strength-
ened and sustained the controlling structure of the
Eight Banners.

International Relations

    Hatachi Masanori has written "On Tribute Trade Be-
tween the Ch'ing and Yi Dynasty Korea: The Rise and Fall
of Cheng Sang"[a] (Tōyō gakuhō 62.3-4). He discusses the
career of Cheng Sang, the Korean tribute envoy to the
Ch'ing, who held monopolistic control over trade (in
Peking) in textiles and other goods and who engaged in
speculative buying and selling. Hatachi argues that because of the sharp reduction of imported Japanese silver
caused by the decline of the Tsushima trade, the Yi

dynasty reduced its trade with the Ch'ing to the lowest
possible level. For this reason, Cheng Sang was dealt
a severe economic blow and went bankrupt.

Yoshida Kin'ichi's article, "On the Peace Negotiations Between Russia and China at Nerchinsk: The Controversy over Golovin's Report"[c] (in Ichiko ronshū) discusses
the process leading to the conclusion of the Treaty of
Nerchinsk (in 1689), which fixed the border between
Russia and China. Yoshida compares the report of
Golovin, Russia's party to the talks, and the diaries
of the two Jesuits who represented the Ch'ing. He shows
that many falsifications can be found in Golovin's report.

Legal History

In his essay, "A General Analysis of the Sources of
Legal Authority in Civil Cases in the Ch'ing Judicial
System"[a] (Tōyōshi kenkyū 40.1), Shiga Shūzō looks at the
"bases of legal authority" in the "cases of litigation"
(t'ing-sung) in the courts of the departments and
counties of the Ch'ing. The standards of judgment in
these cases were "law" (fa), "reason" (li), and "circumstances" (ch'ing) [with the additional connotation of
human feeling]. Of these, the most common standards for
adjudication were "circumstances" and "reason" [often
referred to together as ch'ing-li]. Dynastic regulations
partially served to formalize ch'ing-li, and the appli-
cation of law was adapted to ch'ing-li. Yet, the "bases
of legal authority" in civil cases, Shiga argues, did
not exist apart from statutory law.[23]

Intellectual History

Mizoguchi Yūzō, in his article "Tao and Wen in the
Late Ming"[e] (Tōyō bunka 61), reconsiders the Wang Yang-
ming school of the late Ming by showing that these
scholars denied the conceptual equality and the univer-
sality of fixed principles (ting-li) and adapted principle (li) to the manifold aspects of reality. He

understands their notion of principle to be a manifestation of the self and a recognition of individual diver-
sity. He argues that through a study of one's own life,
human impartial truth (the tao) could be investigated
as human essence or human reality (wen) of an individual
who is not solely defined by universal fixed principles.
Tao runs through wen, and it flows from, or as, wen; tao
and wen are inseparably linked without beginning or end.

Other Work

Sakakura Atsuhide's essay, "On Branch Secretariats
in the Founding Period of the Ming Dynasty"[c] (Jimbun
ronkyū, Kansai Gakuin University 30.4), traces the changes
in Branch Secretariats during the reign of Chu Yüan-chang
in the founding years of the Ming. In 1361 Branch
Secretariats essentially incorporated the Branch Bureaus
of Military Affairs, and came to be in charge not only
of local military and administrative matters but also of
expanding and pacifying new territory. In 1370 Regional
Military Commissions were set up and placed in charge of
military matters, while the Branch Secretariats became
administrative organs of government in fact as well as
in name. These two developments effectively mark the
founding of the Ming dynasty.

Ono Kazuko has written "The Wan-li ti-ch'ao and the
Wan-li shu-ch'ao"[b] (Tōyōshi kenkyū 39.4). She claims that
the Wan-li ti-ch'ao was written by Ch'ien I-pen of the
late Ming, and Ch'ien was related by marriage to Wu Liang,
one of the authors of Wan-li shu-ch'ao. Both men belonged
to the Tung-lin faction, and both books reflect, she
argues, the political position of the Tung-lin.

Finally, we have Watanabe Osamu's "On the Office of
the General Commandant of the Gendarmerie in the Ch'ing"[a]
(Shien, Rikkyō daigaku shigakkai 126). He traces the changes
undergone by the Gendarmerie (charged with keeping the peace
in the capital area, Peking), which was created in 1674 and
lasted through the collapse of the Ch'ing dynasty.

JAPANESE STUDIES OF POST-OPIUM WAR CHINA: 1981

Shimizu Minoru, in
Shigaku zasshi 91.5
(May 1982), 219-26.

Historical research on modern and contemporary
China has entered a new stage since the rapid liberali-
zation of academic intercourse and the recent inundation
of Chinese publications. Ishida Yoneko's essay "Recent
Trends in Chinese Research on the Boxers: Changes in the
Status of Peasant Struggles in Modern Chinese History"[b]
(Chūgoku kenkyū geppō 395) addresses some new developments in recent Chinese studies of modern history. She
makes three points: (a) that there has been an increase
in the number of solid, empirical studies; (b) that a
variety of opposing points of view have been expressed;
and (c) that methodologically they have emphasized the
development of capitalism, with a negative evaluation of
the peasantry and peasant struggles. She expresses her
doubts about this methodology.

In his essay, "The Present State of Affairs in
Modern and Contemporary Historical Research Among Chinese
Historians"[b] (Chikaki ni arite 1), Banno Ryōkichi points
out that among recent trends one may perceive that
scholars from both China and Japan are groping toward
the relative independence of historical science; and
their new orientations in modern history share this consciousness as the scholarly debates unfold. Both Ishida
and Banno question where, under the present situation,
points of scholarly contact and debate will prove
fruitful for modern historical research in China.

Three new journals published inaugural issues this

year: Shingai kakumei kenkyū (Studies on the 1911 Revolution); Chūgoku kindaishi kenkyū (Studies in modern
Chinese history); and Chikaki ni arite: Kin-gendai
Chūgoku o meguru tōron no hiroba (At present, a forum
for debate on modern and contemporary China, ed. Nozawa
Yutaka). These publications amount to the sounding of
a tocsin on individual, scattered research, on the tendency to ever more minute research topics, and on the
blurring of the central issues. These journals are in
touch with the new trends of research in China, and are
asking us such basic questions as: What is modern and
contemporary historical research on China, and why must
it exist? In the paragraphs that follow, I would like
to examine the past year's research, generally pro-
ceeding by historical eras.

The Taiping Movement and the Structure of Power After It
     The following four articles were concerned with
some aspect of the Taiping Rebellion: Nakayama Yoshihiro,
"The Activities of Women in the Taiping Movement"[a] (Kita
Kyūshū daigaku gaikokugo gakubu kiyō 43); Kojima Shinji,
"A Study of the Relationship Between the God-Worshipping
Sect, the God-Worshipping Society, and the Hakka People"[b]
(Chūgoku kindaishi kenkyū 1); Lin Ch'uan-fang, "A Study
of the Sources for 'Goods Words to Admonish the Age'"[a]
(Ryūkoku shidan 79); and Kawabata Genji, "On the King of
Celestial Virtue and the King of Great Peace"[b] (in
Ichiko ronshū).
     Nakayama's analysis of the position of women in
the Taiping Rebellion discusses how women gradually lost
their autonomy through the expansion and resultant
changes when the women's barracks (nü-ying) first became
"women's dormitories" (nü-kuan) and then "sororal
housing" (chieh-mei-kuan), a process that eliminated
their separate organization as a military bloc. The
autonomous role played by women in productive labor has
been much minimized by our emphasis on the family com-

munal nature of the Taipings and their essentially war-
like character.

Kojima elucidates the conditions under which one
would enter the God-Worshipping Sect. He argues that
for the Hakka people freedom from the bonds of kinship
and localism (which centered around worship of the indigenous "gods of the soil and grains" or she-chi) spurred
acceptance of a new monotheistic religion opposed to
idols; this religion became the focal point for a cohesion that transcended village, sex, status, or origin.
As Kojima also recognizes, the extent to which the God-
Worshipping Sect was capable of turning the "conflict
between Hakkas and local people" into an opposition between followers of the God-Worshipping Sect and the
local militia remains a problem.

Lin Ch'uan-fang claims that the "Ch'üan-shih liang-
yen" (Good Words to Admonish the Age)[1] was the "starting
point for the ideology of the Taiping Rebellion." He
provides a valuable analysis of the sources and demonstrates that about 40% of the text was "a Chinese digest
of the Bible," taken from quotations and extracts from
the Chinese translation of the Bible by Robert Morrison
and William Milne.

Kawabata argues that in the early years of the
Taiping movement Europeans were inclined toward the hope
that the Taiping leader, the King of Celestial Virtue,
would become China's new sovereign.

Seven essays were concerned with clarifying the
structure of local control at the time of the Taiping
Rebellion: Usui Sachiko, "Problems of Taxation in Soo-
chow and Sung-chiang Prefectures Before the Taiping
Rebellion"[a] (Shakai keizai shigaku 47.2); Usui Sachiko,
"An Investigation of Land Tax Figures in the Ch'ing
Dynasty: Fluctuations in the Market Exchange Rate of
Silver and Copper, Tax Abatements, the Price of Rice,
Abatement in the Prices for Grain Shipment, and Shifts

in the Tax Burden on Tax-Paying Households in Kiangnan
from the Late Ch'ien-lung Period through T'ung-chih 6
(1867)"[b] (Chūgoku kindaishi kenkyū 1); Natsui Haruki,
"Conditions of Rent Collection in a Landlord Bursary in
Mid-19th Century Soochow: The Rent Reduction of the
T'ung-chih Era and the Process Leading to It"[b] (Shigaku
zasshi 90.7); Kobayashi Yukio, "T'ao Hsü and the 'Chou-
chuang t'uan-lien' in the Period of the Taiping Revolution (1)"[a] (Chūgoku kindaishi kenkyū 1); Fukuda Setsuo,
"Notes on a Study of Hunan in the Ch'ing Dynasty (2): On
the Hung-chiang yü-ying hsiao-shih (1)"[a] (Fukuoka joshi
tandai kiyō 21); Meguro Katsuhiko, "On the Pao-chia
System After the Taiping Rebellion: The Case of Hunan
Province"[c] (Aichi kyōiku daigaku kenkyū hōkoku-Shakai
kagaku 30); and Morita Akira, "A Reinvestigation of
I-t'u[2] in the Ch'ing Dynasty"[e] (Tōyō gakuhō 62.3-4).

Both of Usui's as well as Natsui's articles clarify
in quantitative terms the nature of Chinese social and
economic structure around the time of the Taiping Rebellion. Kobayashi and Fukuda both describe concretely the
local gentry as leaders in local society, and Meguro and
Morita explain the functions that gave substance to the
structure of local gentry control in the late Ch'ing.

In her first article, Usui looks for the historical
causes that required tax and fiscal reform in Chekiang
and Kiangsu after the defeat of the Taipings. She shows
that, for one, there was a considerable increase in the
tax burden for tax-paying households (particularly the
smaller households who paid taxes in copper cash) from
the Tao-kuang reign on, because of the excessive exac-
tion of local government, the decreasing revenues that
accompanied the decline in the prices of rice and raw
cotton, and the relative rise in the importance of silver over copper cash. (Her second essay deals with the
rise in the tax burden from a numerical perspective.)
She also shows that as the inequality of this tax burden

became more apparent, it caused frequent tax revolts.
As a result, "the resident local ruling group (large
households) united with local official power in response
to the antagonism that developed with the direct producers (small households)... Because of their dependence
on local officials to collect taxes, large households
emerged with a new structure in which they gained for
themselves a privileged tax status."

Natsui's essay seeks to clarify the changes in
landlord-tenant relations in Soochow in the mid-19th
century by looking at changes in rent collection by a
landlord bursary (tsu-chan). He goes on to note the
widespread existence of tenant in arrears (wan-tien) in
the 1850's. The upsurge of rent resistance facilitated
the Taiping invasion of Kiangnan, and under Taiping
occupation, past tenancy relations collapsed and a rent
reduction was put into effect. He shows that despite
the official-landlord rent collection structure and the
rent reduction policies after the suppression of the
Taipings, rent collections led to extreme hardship, and
landlord-tenant class antagonism came into the open.

Meguro points out that, because of the local
gentry's direct contact with the workings of the pao-chia
system, there was a "further deepening of local gentry
participation in local politics." Morita treats the
collapse or decline of the i-t'u system during the
Taiping movement as a switch to "a proxy tax collection
structure centered on the influential local gentry." He
claims that this change denoted the active assumption
of control over village structure by the local gentry.

Popular Movements

Two essays that discuss popular movements in the
19th century were: Namiki Yorihisa, "The Nien Rebellion
and Fortified Communities"[c] (Tōyō gakuhō 62.3-4); and
Kanbe Teruo, "The Moslem Rebellion in T'eng-ydeh"[a]
(Ōita daigaku kyōiku gakubu kenkyū kiyō-Jimbun shakai

kagaku 5.6). Through an analysis of fortified communities, Namiki offers a critique of the views of a new
group of scholars (such as Ōta Hideo) who see the Nien
as a rebellion of local bullies. He argues that "the
Nien Rebellion concealed its immanent fruition by undermining [through dismemberment and antagonism] the old
familial order." Kanbe shows that the Moslem regime in
T'eng-yüeh and Ta-li strongly influenced England toward
reopening trade in Burma and Yunnan. Yet, he argues
the need for a comprehensive view of the revolts of
this period -- Taiping, Nien, and various minority
peoples -- and not to see them separately.

Silk Industry, Foreign Commodities, and Chinese Peasantry

Within the structure of the Chinese peasantry's
capacity for self-support, the silk industry (like the
cotton industry) became incorporated into world markets
and was forced to undergo even greater transfigurations
than the cotton industry. The development of the mechanized silk industry through domestic and foreign capital,
beginning in the late 19th century, brought about two
responses among the peasants who worked in both sericulture and the silk industry in Kiangsu and Chekiang: (1)
they now bought the raw cocoons from the factories where
silk was reeled, as in Wu-hsi and Shao-hsing; and (2)
they continued to produce native silk thread themselves,
as in Hu-chou. Suzuki Tomoo has written two essays on
the former issue: "Foreign Capital and the Development
of Cocoon Transactions in Wu-hsi in the Late Ch'ing"[b]
(Tōyō gakuhō 63.1-2); and "The Mechanized Silk Industry
of Shanghai During the Period of the 1911 Revolution
and the Movement of Capital in Silk Thread Manufacture"[c]
(in Shingai hōkoku). Hata Korehito has written an essay
that deals with the latter aspect: "Sericulture in Late
Ch'ing Hu-chou and the Export of Raw Silk Thread"[a] (in
Nakajima ronshū, vol. 2).

Hata argues that what made it possible for Hu-chou
silk thread to continue being produced was: (a) techni-
cal and organizational improvements in the productive
capacity of peasants who supported the rent resistance
trend; and (b) a strengthening of the bonds among those
peasants whose relations had earlier been strained.
Suzuki's first article (on Wu-hsi) relies on analyses
of cocoon transactions from the era under study. He
shows that after the Sino-Japanese War foreign capital
brought together in Wu-hsi the local authorities, the
landlords, the cocoon firms, natively capitalized silk-
thread manufacture, and other commerce in cocoons. He
also demonstrates that these groups formed "an additional
structural layer of repression and exploitation" for
peasant sericulture. Using this framework, Suzuki notes
in his other essay (on the mechanized silk industry in
Shanghai) that the capital invested in local Shanghai
silk thread manufacturing around the time of the 1911
Revolution was merely "an alliance of exploiters dependent" on foreign capital and Ch'ing authority against
peasant sericulture and women laborers in silk thread
manufacture.

On the other hand, Sōda Saburō (in "The Growth of
the Modern Silk Industry in China,"[c] Rekishigaku kenkyū
489) traces the development of local silk manufacturing
in Shanghai in the 1910's by the improvements in domestic
economic conditions. As reasons for improvements he
cites: the rise in wages for women laborers and the formation of educational institutions for them (see also
Sōda's essay, "Conditions for Women Laborers in the Silk
Industry in China,"[d] Chiiki bunka kenkyū 6); the expansion of cocoon firms; the spread of a system of factory
rental; and the shift to native banks (or "money shops")
as holders of money. We now need an overall structure
with which to understand the mechanized silk industry,
one which integrates Suzuki's "semi-colonial" structure

with Sōda's idea of a domestic system of native capital
-- including the linkage between native and foreign
capital, as well as the concrete structure of the earlier
raw silk thread production and its system of exploitation.

Two essays analyzed the links between the structure
of Chinese markets and the influx of foreign commodities:
Kawakatsu Heita, "English Textile and East Asian Markets
in the Late 19th Century"[a] (Shakai keizai shigaku 47.2)
and Miyata Michiaki, "A Study of the Flow of Foreign
Commodities in the Late Ch'ing: Guild Control over the
Movement of Goods"[a] (Sundai shigaku 52). By looking at
the quality of cotton thread in use, Kawakatsu compares
and investigates the problem of Great Britain's inability
to supply directly a substitute for the previously used
East Asian cotton cloth. He goes on to deduce a supply
and demand structure of East Asian-style markets (heavy
thread, thick cloth -- China and Japan), Western-style
markets (fine thread, thin cloth -- England), and mixed
markets (India). He shows that the "existence of East
Asian-style markets in the countries of the Far East
functioned as a kind of 'protective tariff,' a sort of
breakwater before the tidal wave of foreign-capitalized
commodities that came pouring into China en masse." However, I think that the resolution of the conflict and
competition between English and native cotton cloth lay
rather in the structure of (circulation in) these East
Asian-style markets.

This latter point is suggested by Miyata. He argues
that the flow of foreign trade commodities to the Chinese
interior was controlled at all levels of a structure of
circulation in which commercial guilds overlapped one
another and at the pinnacle stood a "foreign trade
guild" (of Chinese merchants) at the treaty ports. This
guild structure and its superiority in pricing prevented
foreign merchants from penetrating domestic markets.

Intellectual History

A number of essays discuss the personal world of
individuals active in the period from the era of early
Westernization (yang-wu) through the 1898 Reform Move-
ment: Hatano Yoshihiro, "Tso Tsung-t'ang's Personality:
A Look at His Family Letters"[a] (in Ichiko ronshū); Enoki
Kazuo, "Tung Hsün and His Writings: Particularly His
Diary (5)"[a] (Kindai Chūgoku 9); Kamachi Noriko, "Huang
Tsun-hsien's Views on Reform"[a] (in Ichiko ronshū);
Fujioka Kikuo, "Chang Chien and the Examination System"[a]
(Hōgaku kenkyū, Hokkai gakuen daigaku hōgakkai 16.3).
Each of these articles makes use of diaries, letters,
chronological biographies, or personal writings as a
means of relating each individual to their history. They
were all men who stemmed the tide of violent change
within the system in the latter half of the 19th century.
There should be a commonality in their having lived at
the same time that transcends their individuality, as
well as a temporal proclivity shared by men grounded in
the same society. We need a demonstration of their
individual natures, based on this issue.

Gotō Nobuko has written "K'ang Yu-wei's View of the
World of Great Harmony: The Structure of Its Existence
and Its Importance in Intellectual History"[b] (Shinshū
daigaku jimbun kagaku ronshū 15). She argues that K'ang
Yu-wei's structure for the world of Great Harmony, based
on "human equality and the principle of autonomy," constituted "a way for all men to stand on their own under
heaven, as sons of heaven, and to be equals as comrades."
She sees this as "a new ideal forcing traditional Confucianism one step further back." We can see K'ang not
having completely eliminated tradition, continually strug-
gling in contradictions and rivalries with the past.

A similar process was at work in the bank debate
that is analyzed by Hamashita Takeshi, "The 'Bank Debate'
and the Establishment of the Imperial Bank of China in

the Late Ch'ing: Criticisms and Revisions of Sheng Hsüan-
huai's Construction Plan of 1897"[c] (Hitotsubashi ronsō
85.6). The debate demonstrates the volatile and bitter
process whereby the traditional economic structure and
a modern economic structure were joined.

Fukazawa Hideo analyzes the 1898 Reform Movement
from the angles of intellectual and socio-economic
history in his three essays: "The 1898 Reform Movement
and Hsiang-pao"[a] (in Nakajima ronshū, vol. 2); "The 1898
Reform Movement and the [Hsiang-pao] Newspaper Office"[b]
(Shūkan Tōyōgaku 45); and "The Social and Economic Background to the 1898 Reform Movement: A Look at Hunan
Province"[c] (Rekishi to bunka, Iwate University). Also,
Arita Kazuo's article "A Study of the I-chiao ts'ung-
pien"[b] (Tōkyō gaikokugo daigaku ronshū 31) analyzes anti-
reformist thought as one part of the intellectual atmos-
phere of the 1898 Reform Movement.

On Debates in the People's Republic of China

A number of essays introduced the debates of the
1980 Academic Conference on the History of the Boxer
Movement held in Chinan: Satō Kimihiko, "The Debate over
the'Evaluation' of the Boxers"[b] (Chūgoku kenkyū geppō
398); Kobayashi Kazumi, "Ideas on the 'Evaluation' of the
Boxer Movement: Thoughts During My First Trip to China
for the Academic Conference on the History of the Boxer
Movement, Held to Commemorate the Eightieth Anniversary
of the Boxers"[c] (Chūgoku kenkyū geppō 398); and Kobayashi
Kazumi, "The Principles Governing the Boxer Movement: An
Evaluation of Chinese Scholars' View of the Boxers'
Limitations -- 'No Organization and No Leadership'"[d]
(Shingai kakumei kenkyū 1). They point out that most
of the areas of debate concentrated on external, phenom-
enal "evaluations." To the extent that Chinese studies
of the Boxers, studies that are fitted to the "bits and
pieces of the formula" of the materialist conception of
history, devolve on studies of origins and genealogies,

Kobayashi criticizes them for being unable theoretically
to comprehend the Boxers' "communitarian reconstruction
movement for popular defense" and "the principles of the
[Boxer] movement."

The 1911 Revolution and Its Times

A number of essays dealt with themes concerning the
period of the 1911 Revolution in the areas of popular
movements, the revolutionary parties, economic activities,
and intellectuals. Each of the following four articles
discusses the role played by secret societies in popular
movements: Hata Korehito, "Rural Society in Chekiang
During the Emergence of Imperialism: T'ai-chou Bandits
and the Revolutionaries in Chekiang and Kiangsu"[b]
(Rekishigaku kenkyū, special issue); Shimizu Minoru, "The
1911 Revolution and Popular Movements in Hunan"[b] (in
Shingai hōkoku); Katō Naoko, "Popular Movements in Shantung During the Period of the 1911 Revolution"[a] (Shiron
34); and Kojima Yoshio, "Secret Societies in the Kiangsu
and Chekiang Area in the Early Republic"[b] (in Nakajima
ronshū, vol. 2).

Hata clarifies the process through which local
bandits in T'ai-chou, while undergoing "qualitative
transformation," organized into secret societies and then
coalesced into a revolutionary party. He calls these
bandits and secret societies the "middle stratum that
formed a circuit back into village society." Because
this quality in them was the point of contact with the
revolutionaries, this contact could not, he argues, be
a circuit for the expression of popular revolution in fact.

Shimizu argues that the popular mass struggles in
Hunan were characterized by a secret society organization
and by cooperation with local revolutionaries. By tracing the subjective response toward revolution by the
allied secret society groups, Shimizu offers a high evaluation of their capacity to cut open a path toward the
overthrow of the Ch'ing dynasty. In contrast to Shimizu,

Kojima uses documents concerning the activities of the
Chung-kuo min-kuo kung-chin-hui to demonstrate that
secret societies around the time of the revolution possessed a dual nature. The method by which he evaluates
this dual nature within the development of an actual movement should be used in studying other popular movements.

Essays concerned with the revolutionaries include:
Matsumoto Takehiko, "The Importance of the Hsing Chung
Hui in Sun Yat-sen's Revolutionary Movement, with Special
Reference to Overseas Chinese"[a] (Kindai Chūgoku 9);
Nakamura Tetsuo, "The Influence Exercised by Kemuyama
Sentarō's Kinsei museifushugi [Modern anarchism] on the
Revolutionary Movement"[b] (in Shingai hōkoku); Hanzawa
Junta, "The Political Process Leading to the Uprising of
T'ang Ts'ai-ch'ang's Independence Army: The Development
of the Chinese Revolutionary Party from the Boxer Inci-
dent to the Russo-Japanese War"[a] (Gunji shigaku 16.4);
and Kojima Yoshio, "The Chinese National Assembly and
the 1911 Revolution"[c] (in Shingai hōkoku).

On the basis of class differentiation of the overseas Chinese of Yokohama, Matsumoto shows that the activities of the revolutionaries during the Hsing Chung Hui
period were concentrated in Yokohama in the organization
of the Chung-ho-t'ang, which was composed of lower class
workers. Nakamura calls attention to the fact that the
Narodnaya Volya[3] position introduced by Kemuyama Sentarō
and primarily concerned with people's rights continued
in fact to exist even after the founding of the T'ung-
meng-hui, despite internal discord. Kojima argues that
the enlightened activities for national salvation and
revolution by the Chinese National Assembly, which was
organized before the Canton uprising of 1911, played a
major role in accelerating the independence movements of
other provinces after the Wuchang uprising. I think it
is fair to say that each of these essays examines previously unexplored territory.

In the field of economic history, we have: Kurahashi
Masanao, "The Bankruptcy of Tung-sheng-ho, One of the
Great Merchant Houses in Ying-k'ou"[b] (Tōyō gakuhō 63.1-2);
Hamashita Takeshi, "China and International Monetary
Relations Around the Time of the 1911 Revolution: The
Decline in the Value of Silver and Reforms of the Monetary
System"[d] (in Shingai hōkoku); and Watanabe Atsushi, "The
Move Toward Reform of the Salt Administration in Modern
China: The Chiu-ta Pure Salt Company"[d] (Kumamoto daigaku
kyōiku gakubu kiyō-Jimbun kagaku 30).

Kurahashi argues that the local panic that arose in
Ying-k'ou [an important Manchurian port--JAF] in 1907
was due to the contradiction between old-type economic
policies symbolized by kuo-lu-yin[4] and rapid advances
made in the scale of the economy during the Kuang-hsü
reign. As a result, there emerged a new type of economic
policy, but he does not specify its content. Hamashita
attempts to uncover the formation and deepening of an
international monetary network around the time of the
1911 Revolution by looking at developments aimed at re-
forming the monetary systems of those Asian nations
using silver coins and at unifying their currencies
through the intermediaries of colonial banks, this at a
time when the value of silver was changing drastically
early in the 20th century. Watanabe discusses the opposition between the "reformist bourgeoisie," on the one
hand, and the salt merchants and militarists, on the
other, over the modernization of the salt industry from
1911 to 1927. He argues that in order to understand the
nature of the Chiu-ta Company and the "reformist bourgeoisie" we need to know about the people who participated in the meetings concerning the salt administration
that was the Chiu-ta's base of influence.

Two other studies that fill lacunae in research on
the 1911 Revolution are: Kawamoto Kunie, "The Việt Nam
Quang Phục Hội and the 1911 Revolution"[a] (in Shingai

hōkoku); and Nakami Tatsuo, "The 1911 Revolution and the
Mongols"[a] (in Shingai hōkoku). Kawamoto argues that the
success of the 1911 Revolution caused an intellectual
shift from constitutional monarchy to republicanism in
the Vietnamese independence movement. Nakami claims that
the 1911 Revolution served as a "catalyst" for the Mongolian independence movement and offered the possibility
for the ethnic reunification of the Mongolian people as
well as a revival of their political sovereignty.

Two essays discuss Sung Chiao-jen: Matsumoto Hideki,
"The Formation of the Provisional Constitution of the
Republic of China and Sung Chiao-jen"[b] (Ritsumeikan
shigaku 2); and Katakura Yoshikazu, "On the Assassination
of Sung Chiao-jen"[a] (Shisō, Nihon daigaku shigakka 27).
Matsumoto argues that Sung's fierce debate with Sun Yat-
sen over the national polity unfolded in the discussions
concerning the provisional O-chou [Hupeh] constitution,
the master plan for the organization of the provisional
government, and the provisional state constitution. However, Sung finally realized his goal within the crisis
compelling a policy to deal with Yüan Shih-k'ai.

In his analysis of Wang Ching-wei, Kusunose Masaaki
("Wang Ching-wei's 'Nationalism' in the Era of the 1911
Revolution,"[b] Shigaku kenkyū 152) argues that although
Wang's reformist views involved the principle of trans-
forming the imperial system, they cannot be called
bourgeois revolutionary thought.

Many empirical essays were concerned with Sun Yat-
sen, such as: Takahashi Yoshikazu, "The Importance of
the Decisive Rupture Between Sun Yat-sen and Huang Hsing
at the Time of the Formation of the Chinese Revolutionary
Party"[a] (Nagoya daigaku Tōyōshi kenkyū hōkoku 7); Ikeda
Makoto, "On Sun Yat-sen's Notion of 'Ruling the Nation
with the Party': His Expectations of a 'Government by
All the People' by Balancing of Rights and Abilities"[b]
(Ritsumeikan hōgaku 150-154); Fujii Shōzō, "Sun Yat-sen

and His [Idea of a] 'Sino-Japanese Alliance' at the Time
of the Twenty-One Demands"[a] (in Ichiko ronshū); Kubota
Bunji, "Sun Yat-sen's Idea of 'Ceding Manchuria and Mon-
golia'"[c] (in Nakajima ronshū, vol. 2); Kubota Hiroko,
"The Meeting of Sun Yat-sen and Soong Ching-ling"[a] (in
Nakajima ronshū, vol. 2); and Kubota Bunji and Kubota
Hiroko, "On the Date of the Marriage of Sun Yat-sen to
Soong Ching-ling"[a] (Shingai kakumei kenkyū 1).

    Takahashi's analysis of the background to the Sun-
Huang opposition concludes that while Sun, facing defeat
in the second revolution, conceived of the Chinese Revolutionary Party as overcoming and transcending the structure of the T'ung-meng-hui, Huang advocated a return to
the origins of the T'ung-meng-hui. Ikeda locates in the
early Republican period the root of Sun's idea of "ruling
the nation with the party," and he notes that after 1921
there was a shift toward "democratic" (min-chih-chu-i)
party politics based on the earlier notion of two great
parties in Western nations. Fujii demonstrates the
authenticity of Sun Yat-sen's [desire for a] "Sino-Japanese
alliance" and his "letter to Koike Chōzō"; while Kubota
Bunji shows that Sun's concept of "ceding Manchuria and
Mongolia" never took shape, and does so by critically
examining sources concerning Uchida Ryōhei and Mori Kaku
whose ideas were considered the basis of this notion.
The last two essays by the Kubotas explode a commonly
held theory by firmly establishing the dates (in 1892
and 1913) of the meetings of Sun Yat-sen and Soong Chia-
shu and Soong Ching-ling, and of Sun's wedding (in 1915).
All of these articles are important for they enhance
our increasingly accurate picture of Sun.

    A fair number of essays investigate rural village
society in the 1911 period: Nishikawa Masao, "A Look at
the Local Gazetteer of Chien-yang County, Szechwan"[a]
(Kanazawa daigaku bungakubu ronshū shigakka hen 1);
Morita Akira, "Reforms in Water Utilization Organization

in the Early Republic"[f] (in Satō ronshū); Hamaguchi
Nobuko, "On Mi Feng-chi: A Rural Village Leader in the
Late Ch'ing and Early Republic"[a] (in Ichiko ronshū);
Nakamura Jihee, "On Clans Feuds in the Villages of
Kwangtung in the Early Republic: From the Annual Report
of P'u-lo County"[b] (in Ichiko ronshū); and Hayashi Kazuo,
"Commercial Centers in Central and South China in the
Republican Period"[b] (Jimbun, Kyōto daigaku kyōyōbu 27).

Nishikawa painstakingly traces the genealogies and
activities of the Chien-yang gentry, with diligent reference to the local gazetteer, in order to clarify the
historical nature of the newly risen gentry ruling group
who made political, economic, and social advances in the
late Ch'ing and Republican period. We can see here one
apsect of the "anti-revolutionary" position against the
1911 Revolution supported at the base of rural society.
Morita examines the process through which the local gentry were subsumed under official authority through the
reforms in the organization of water utilization. While
Hamaguchi looks at one case of the multi-faceted existence
of the local gentry, Nakamura examines cases of clan
feuds, and Hayashi elucidates the function and structure
of the commercial population centers that were the central villages of the late Ch'ing. Discussion of this
"politically tumultuous period" -- the era of the 1911
Revolution -- at its social and economic foundations
is of no small significance.

The May Fourth and New Culture Movements

A goodly number of essays were concerned with issues
from the period of the May Fourth Movement. Nozawa
Yutaka ("Rice Riots and the May Fourth Movement: Mutual
Relations Between the Peoples and States of East Asia,"[d]
Chikaki ni arite 1) offers a perspective worth studying.
He examines the rice riots in terms of the changes in
the overall circulation of rice in East Asia and the
influence this exerted on China in the May Fourth period.

In the area of popular movements, Itoi Reiko
("Women's Liberation and the May Fourth Movement: The
Case of Tientsin,"[a] Shikai 28) analyzes the women's movement in Tientsin. Takatsuna Hirofumi ("Labor Conditions
in the Kailan Coal Mines and the Workers' Disputes of
1922,"[a] Rekishigaku kenkyū 491) analyzes the objective
conditions experienced by mine workers there and their
level of consciousness as the makers of change. Kasahara
Tokuji ("Disputes over Educational Funds for State-
Sponsored Schools in Peking: One Form of Anti-Warlordism
in the Early 1920's,"[b] in Nakajima ronshū, vol. 2) and
Nakamura Tadashi ("The June First Incident in Changsha,"[b]
in Nakajima ronshū, vol. 2) both clarify the progression toward the May Fourth Movement.

In the intellectual history of this era, Kondō
Kuniyasu's "Yang Ch'ang-chi and Mao Tse-tung: 'Native
Philosophy' of the Young Mao"[a] (Shakai kagaku kenkyū,
Tōkyō daigaku shakai kagaku kenkyūjo 33.4) points out
that in his early years Mao learned from Yang Ch'ang-
chi's ideas a method of interiorizing social and political concerns as philosophy. Fujitani Hiroshi ("The
Acceptance and Development of Marxism in China,"[a] Handai
hōgaku 116, 117) examines the nature of Marxism in this
early period through the works of Li Ta-chao. Kobayashi
Yoshifumi's "Huang Yen-p'ei and the Movement for Voca-
tional Education"[a] (Tōyōshi kenkyū 39.4) is a painstaking study that opens up a field as yet unstudied.

International Relations
Katō Yūzō ("Taishō and Min-kuo: China around 1920,"[b]
Shisō 689) looks into the changes among Chinese and
Japanese intellectuals wrought by the Twenty-One Demands.
Yamamoto Shirō ("One Side of Sino-Japanese Relations at
the Time of the Terauchi Cabinet: Nishihara Kamezō and
Banzai Rihachirō,"[a] Shirin 64.1) and Harada Keiichi
("The Movement to Boycott Japanese Goods and the Plan
for the Establishment of a Sino-Japanese Bank: The

Position of the Osaka Bourgeoisie in the 1910's,"[a]
Hisutoria 90) both discuss Japanese responses to events
in China. Sasaki Toshiko ("Policies Concerning the Preservation of the Chinese Government's Independence: 1912-
1922,"[a] Kokusai kankeigaku kenkyū, Tsūdajuku daigaku
kiyō 7) deals with the issues of the responses of Yüan
Shih-k'ai, Tuan Ch'i-jui, and Hsü Shih-ch'ang to the
protection or independence of China. Hanzawa Junta
("Sun Yat-sen's Acceptance of the Communists and Japan's
Response,"[b] Seiji keizai shigaku 181) discusses the
policies of Soviet Russia, Japan, America, and England
with respect to China.

Other Work

        Sasaki Masaya's essay "A Study of the Opium War:
From the English Army's Attack at Canton to the Dismissal
of Elliot as Plenipotentiary (5)"[a] (Kindai Chūgoku 9)
focuses on the benefits of the San-yüan-li Incident.
Tagawa Kōzō's "The Problem of Displaced Koreans Crossing
the [Chinese] Border in the Early Kuang-hsü Era"[a] (in
Ichiko ronshū) discusses the issue of immigrant Koreans
returning to the Chien-tao area. Nagai Kazumi ("The
Monarchical Restoration Incident of 1917 and Liang Ch'i-
ch'ao,"[a] Shinshū daigaku jimbun kagaku ronshū 15) deals
with the activities of Chang Hsün. Yamane Yukio's "The
Founding and Development of the Tōhō bunka gakuin"[e] (in
Ichiko ronshū) discusses the role this organization
played in Japanese studies of East Asia. Nakami Tatsuo
("The Morrison Documents at Present,"[b] Tōyō bunko shohō
12) introduces the present state of the Morrison collection held in the Mitchell Library, Sydney, Australia.

        Several books have attempted to describe the
historical realities of modern China: Horikawa Tetsuo,
Chūgoku kindai no seiji to shakai (Modern Chinese politics
and society)[a]; Nohara Shirō, Masui Tsuneo, et al., Chūgoku
bunkashi: Kindaika to dentō (The cultural history of

China: Modernization and tradition)[a]; and Shibahara
Takuji, <u>Nihon kindaika no sekaishi teki ichi, sono
hōhōron teki kenkyū</u> (The place in world history of the
modernization of Japan: A methodological study).[a]
These books are each worthy of separate reviews.

8

MING-CH'ING STUDIES IN JAPAN: 1982

Ueda Makoto, in
Shigaku zasshi 92.5
(May 1983), 193-99.

The new scholarly trends first apparent in the past
two or three years took concrete shape in works written
in 1982. One of these trends was enhanced academic exchange with the People's Republic of China. Symbolic of
this development was the collection of essays contributed
to the International Academic Symposium on Ming and
Ch'ing History convened at Nankai University in August
1980: Ming-Ch'ing shih kuo-chi hsüeh-shu t'ao-lun-hui
lun-wen-chi. There has also been a noticeable increase
in the Chinese scholarly world of interest in Japanese
research. An essay by Hamashima Atsutoshi was published
in a Chinese journal (see below), and we have also heard
that the nei-pu ("internal circulation only") journal
Chung-kuo shih yen-chiu tung-t'ai has introduced trends
in Japanese scholarship as well as exerpted and translated several Japanese essays.

Furthermore, opportunities for Japanese researchers
to peruse materials held in China have substantially increased, and welcome indeed are developments toward the
sharing of historical documents, as manifested for example by Hamashima Atsutoshi's "A Brief Introduction to
the An Wu ch'in-shen hsi kao, Held in the Peking Library"[g]
(Hokkaidō daigaku bungakubu kiyō 30.1). By the same
token, there has been heightened interchange in the form
of Chinese scholars spending extended periods in Japan.
Last year Fu I-ling, the renowned social and economic
historian, visited Kyoto, and Chou Yüan-lien, a special-

ist in Ch'ing history, visited Tokyo. One concrete result of Chou's stay was the publication of his essay,
"The Ch'ing Imperial Clan"[a] (Gakujutsu kokusai kōryu
sankō shiryōshū, Meiji University 80). At present many
Japanese students are pursuing research at various uni-
versities in China; they are also learning about Chinese
realities first-hand. If those who have established
close ties with Chinese scholars publish their research
in the next few years, then Japanese sinology will be
immeasurably advanced.

Two recent scholarly trends have been: the summing
up of studies done in the 1970's (work regarding the
nature of the Chinese gentry would be a representative
example) that developed the theory of historical stages
with particulars from China's actual historical development; and the emergence of methods fundamentally different from that of theory of stages of development. Concerning the former, Hamashima Atsutoshi's essay in
Gendai rekishigaku no seika to kadai (Achievements and
topics of contemporary historiography) summarizes the
results of Japanese research in the 1970's concerning
the issue of kyōdōtai or "community." A leader in the
field of social and economic history throughout the
1970's, Hamashima also published the volume Mindai Kōnan
nōson shakai no kenkyū (Studies in Kiangnan rural society
in the Ming dynasty).[h] On the basis of earlier work, he
systematically describes issues such as water utilization
practices, the equitable field-equitable labor service
system, and popular rebellion. Iwama Kazuo has similarly published a book in an area straddling the fields of
intellectual and social-economic history, Chūgoku no
hōken teki sekaizō (China's feudalistic world view).[c]
It is hoped that both volumes will elicit reviews.

Of the two scholarly trends mentioned above, the
latter both criticizes methods based on a theory of
class struggle and developmental stages as well as

supports a method that might be termed "structural understanding." The undermining of trust in the theory
of stages of societal development is consistent with the
general state of contemporary thought. The present age
is one that cannot be dealt with by 19th century theories
of development. Criticism of such theories is levelled
less from a Marxist perspective than from the position
elaborated by A. G. Frank as "the development of under-
development." This critique also argues that the contemporary period is one that threatens the existence of
mankind itself (a "core" that exists symbolically with
our relation to any system, and in everyday life mankind
becomes ever more controlled and quantified). Under
such circumstances we are faced with the task of finding
a line of approach or a method of historiography that
will relativize, as well as offer a critical perspective
on, the contemporary world. Relativizing the contemporary
era both recognizes the existence of societies fundamentally different from modern and recent societies, and it
is advanced through the work of comparing these different
societies with present society. For this reason, three
things are required: (a) abandonment of past methods that
use a modern framework to judge in a functionalist manner
the societies and cultures thought to be qualitatively
different; (b) recognition of the value of societies and
cultures themselves as objects of study; and (c) elucidation of their intrinsic, internal realm--i.e., structures.

Let us look at Mori Masao, a scholar in search of
a new methodology and keenly aware of the limitations of
a method based on class analysis and stages of development. Mori served as one of the sponsors of a symposium
on Chinese history held in August 1981 in Nagoya, and he
made the keynote report, published as "The Perspective
of Local Society in Studies of Pre-Modern Chinese History:
Keynote Report of the Symposium, Local Society and Leadership"[j] (Nagoya daigaku bungakubu kenkyū ronshū 83).

Last year the papers were published as Chiiki shakai no shiten (The perspective of local society).

In his report Mori describes the need to regard consciousness as an object for research in confronting today's issues. He argues that we cannot organize or resolve issues on the basis of concern for a consciousness of [social] order using the methods of class analysis. Secondly, he stipulates the methodological concept of "local society" (chiiki shakai) by which he means the local arena under a common social order and integrated by a common leadership; and which is different in dimension from such concrete concepts as administrative unit or local area. He argues that four scholarly positions have been advanced in answer to the question of the rôle played by local society as a methodological concept in pre-modern Chinese history -- as the axis of the family and the clan, as a form for landlord supervision, as a form for literati supervision, and as the axis of the state -- and he notes the problem areas in each of these. Mori goes on to examine this general selection of issues with a study of the late Ming period.

The issues he raises were not fully understood by the other participants in the symposium. Mori himself is half to blame for this confusion. The framework of "local society" is not absolutely essential when focusing on the consciousness of [social] order. Mori's true meaning can be seen in his statement at the conference -- that is, his understanding that one segment of the literati whose activities aimed at effective government and aid to the people (ching-shih chi-min) betokened the emergence of a "sense of responsibility that both the ruling class and the ruled class be regulated by a common social order and that they adhere to a common pledge."

One who understands a basic understanding of this view is Kishimoto (née Nakayama) Mio. She wants to know the consciousness on which men of the past based their

actions. She claims that we cannot extrapolate from a
knowledge of class relations to answer this query because
the problem forms its own independent terrain. As we
shall examine later, she has reached this understanding
after wrestling with an explanation for China's intrinsic structure.

One cause of this symposium's lack of unity is that
no theoretical bridge is offered to link "local society"
as a methodological construct with reality. To construct a bridge, we need to separate "local society" in
which "reproduction" is maintained by a social structure
that regards leadership as an important constituent element from the local framework (such as the administrative unit) established for the resident populace primarily by outside forces [i.e., the central government
--JAF]. Also, we have to describe the points at which
the arena of the former underwent change.

Fuma Susumu offers a suggestion in his essay,
"Popular Uprisings at the End of the Ming and the Sheng-
yüan: The Formation of Public Opinion in Kiangnan Cities
and the Role of the Sheng-yüan"[c] (in Chiiki shakai no
shiten). Using upheavals and riots of scholars at the
end of the Ming, Fuma shows that they influenced each
other and that from the middle of the Ming sheng-yüan
emerge at the creators of public opinion at the hsien
or county unit. We can see the hsien, which prior to
the mid-Ming was merely a local [bureaucratic] framework, changing later in the Ming into "local society."
If we were to carry this position further, I think we
can grasp the social upheavals in the late Ch'ing and
Republican eras as a process of transformation into "local society" (with the appearance of a provincial gentry).

Among the other contribution to the symposium was
Taniguchi Kikuo, "Crisis in a North Chinese Rural Vil-
lage at the End of the Ming and One Member of the Local
Gentry: The Case of Lü K'un."[d] By focusing on Lü K'un,

Taniguchi tries to elucidate the issues involved in the
"background to the outbreak of rebellion," as he termed
it in an earlier essay ("A Study of Peasant Rebellions
in the Late Ming,"[c] Ōsaka daigaku kyōyōbu kenkyū shūroku
29 [1980]). He argues that the problem of privileged
corvée exemption (yu-mien)[2] that lay at the base of
North China's crisis was not resolved by the local gentry.

Taniguchi pursues this issue raised at the symposium in another essay, "An Explanation of the Rebellions
of Li Tzu-ch'eng and Chang Hsien-chung"[e] (in Chūgoku
minshū hanran shi, vol. 3). In this piece he recognizes
in Li Tzu-ch'eng's "land equalization" slogan a movement
toward the resolution of the land problem, and he sees
the undermining of the social order as caused by a large
number of chü-jen who participated in Li's peasant military regime.

Hamashima Atsutoshi also contributed an essay to the
Chiiki shakai no shiten, "The Transformation of Local
Society in Kiangnan and Public Authority: On the Formation of 'Shops.'"[i] He develops his arguments further in
an article entitled "A Study of Shops and Rent Resistance
and Rent Arrears in the Southeastern Provinces in the
Late Ming"[j] (in the Chinese journal, Chung-kuo she-hui
ching-chi shih yen-chiu 3 [1982]). He criticizes Mori's
methodology and argues that, as a result of changes in
the structure of land ownership in the late Ming, landlords were no longer able to cope with the lack of rent
payments by themselves. Using jails known as "shops"
(p'u), officials took into custody the poor peasants
accused by the landlords of being guilty of failure to
pay rent. Thus, Hamashima advocates the utility of the
class struggle perspective.

Yoshio Hiroshi's piece for the symposium -- "Roving
Bandits and Local Society in the Late Ming: A Look at
Bandits' 'Spies'"[b] -- was published earlier as an arti-
cle, "Bandits' Spies in the Late Ming"[a] (Nagoya daigaku

Tōyōshi kenkyū hōkoku 7).[3]

Two essays by Inoue Tōru are mutually complementary:
"The Reorganization of the Social Order on the Right
Bank of the Pearl River Delta of Kwangtung and the Role
of the Local Gentry"[a] (in Chiiki shakai no shiten) and
"Insurrections of She-tsei and T'u-tsei[4] on the Right
Bank of the Pearl River Delta of Kwangtung in the Late
Ming and Early Ch'ing"[b] (Shirin 65.5). In the first
article he points out the dual nature of the local gentry -- as maintainers of the social order in local
society and as seekers of personal gain. He argues that
in the late Ming period it was their latter role in
confiscating sand flats and seizing produce from the
land that prompted the confrontation between them and
the general body of landholders. In the second essay,
he claims that the revolts of she-tsei, who rose under
the circumstances described above, were not simply
nu-pien (bondservant uprisings)[5] but had a rent resistance aspect and were joined by tenants and members of
the lower strata of the population. He shows that they
developed in solidarity with t'u-tsei. Basing himself
on Mori's research of recent years, Inoue strives to
bring together within his field of vision the diverse
quality of she-tsei disturbances and the conditions for
rebellion or the undermining of the social order.
Limitations in the historical materials, however, leave
this equation incomplete.

Kishimoto Mio is a scholar concerned explicitly
with structural comprehension. Her essay "On the Decline in the Price of Grain in the K'ang-hsi Era: One
Aspect of Early Ch'ing Economic Thought"[c] (Tōyō bunka
kenkyūjo kiyō 89), while based on two of her earlier
works on commodity prices,[6] clearly states her methodology and includes numerous suggestions for economic and
intellectual history. First, she verifies the drop in
commodity prices that transpired during the K'ang-hsi

reign. With this as a root cause, a decline in the
amount of silver in circulation and a retrenchment policy (with the early Ch'ing government's sea ban) led to
a decline in the value of silver circulating among the
people. Next, she divides the early Ch'ing economic
countermeasures to this slump into four categories:
discontinuance of silver usage, importation of silver,
etc. She argues that they all identified effective demand with currency. This identification emerged because
markets at that time were not closed "limited markets"
but were specialized produce markets primarily aimed at
satisfying external demand, and such demand was understood as the inflow of currency (silver) from outside.
Furthermore, she analyzes in depth the different points
of economic theory of those favoring the abandonment of
silver (such as Huang Tsung-hsi).

One issue this essay raises is that Kishimoto's
theory of open markets provides a strong critique of the
theory of the sprouts of capitalism, and is the reverse
of the theory of limited markets put forth by the school
of Ōtsuka Hisao.[7] If Kishimoto's conception of markets
cannot effectively explain the economic activities of
the people at that time and China's own economic development, then it can have no positive significance. In order to comprehend the structure of her theory statically
we must look outside the structure for causes of social
upheaval. The latter is a flaw common to structuralism.
It cannot be resolved by expanding the range of a structure, by bringing external factors in as internal to the
structure; and then, once having reached this point,[8]
by continuing this operation again. Among other things,
her view that the Ch'ing's control over trade maintained
the centripetal quality of the Chinese economy demonstrates
a tendency in her article to understand the entire Ch'ing
state on the basis of a single economic structure.

In his essay, "The Reorganization and the Nature of

the Status of Servants and Hired Laborers in the Late
Ming and Early Ch'ing"[a] (Tōyōshi kenkyū 41.3), Takahashi
Yoshirō criticizes sharply stages-of-development studies
concerning laws of status. He is referring to works
that argue that the legal reforms concerning status in
the late Ming and early Ch'ing directly reflect the
liberation of people of dependent status and that these
reforms were brought about by the development of productive forces. In fact, these studies assume liberation
from the reforms. He begins by explaining the legal
concepts supporting the statuses of servants and hired
laborers. The former, he argues, was a de jure, absolute status fixed under the ruling order of the state;
the latter was a de facto, relative status by which
state authority legally recognized people as personal
dependents who could be bought and sold. In the early
Ming the principle of rulership was directed at control
over the common people as a homogeneous body to be
managed only on the basis of their families' labor power;
and sought to put a halt to the rise of personal, sub-
ordinating ties among the common people. The New Regulations of the Wan-li reign period renounced this principle and officially authorized possession of "other
men's labor power."

Reforms in the status of servants in the early
Ch'ing advanced one step further by sanctioning the en-
servicement of ordinary commoners through alienation.
Thus, the legal status of servants was made relative
and de facto just like that of hired laborers. Takahashi
sees reforms in the status of hired laborers as techni-
cal adjustments to establish a compatible standard for
regulating the status of employed laborers. I would
like to know why changes were implemented in the legal
conception of status from the late Ming on. Did the
possession of servant labor cause a rapid development
and compromise the law at this time? Or, did a new con-

cept different from the principle of rulership in the
early Ming become firmly established? (If we assume the
former position, we become engulfed once again in a notion of stages of development). It is hoped that subsequent studies will address such issues as whether the
native legal concept underpinning dependent status
among the Manchu ethnic group influenced the laws of
status in the Ch'ing dynasty.

Structural comprehension proved efficacious in
studies of religion as well. Let us first look at the
problems of past research into Chinese religion by
drawing on Sōda Hiroshi's review (in Tōyōshi kenkyū 41.2)
of a book by Tanaka Issei, Chūgoku saishi engeki kenkyū
(A study of ritual theater in China).[a] After reviewing
in detail the theoretical structure of Tanaka's major
work, Sōda argues that the point of the book -- that
"culture based on territorial society (chien shakai) is
continually being both stripped and absorbed by consanguineal society (ketsuen shakai)"-- brilliantly hits on
an important perspective for understanding the uniqueness of Chinese history. We can see, however, when we
look at Sōda's summary that the overall design of the
book plots territorial groupings as made up of common
people while consanguineal groups as the rulers and
landlords, and this view appears to be a rehashing of
class theory.

In many instances, studies of clans, which draw
from the well dug by Professor Niida Noboru, follow this
schema. To the extent, however, that clans are groups
that transcend families and comprise "living communities" (seikatsu kyōdōtai), they must take form as the
level of territorial relations and, thus, territorial
groupings ought to be integrated structurally with consanguineal ones (such as clans). In order to clarify
such a structure, Katayama Tsuyoshi examines lineage
organization in relation to the tax structure and to

the recognition of land ownership. His two essays --
"The T'u-chia-piao and Problems Surrounding It for the
Pearl River Delta of Kwangtung in the Late Ch'ing: Land
Taxes, Household Registers, and Lineage"[a] (Shigaku
zasshi 91.4); "On the T'u-chia System in the Pearl
River Delta of Kwangtung During the Ch'ing: Land Taxes,
Household Registers, and Lineage"[b] (Tōyō gakuhō 63.3-4)
-- are epoch-making studies. These two pieces represent
an attempt to analyze the t'u-chia system, which corre-
sponded to the li-chia system in effect elsewhere in
China, using the t'u-chia-piao which had been inserted
in local gazetteers and genealogies for the Pearl River
delta in the late Ch'ing and Republican eras, and to
illuminate the structure of local society there for the
Ming and Ch'ing. His main points are as follows: (a)
all "households" (hu) were taxation units for a single
lineage or for the entire body of its branches and were
not individual families as living units; (b) actual landowners were seen as individual tax-payers beneath the
tsung-hu (equivalent to the household of the li-chang
under the li-chia system), and they paid taxes to officials through the tsung-hu, and officials did not have
the landowners directly within their control; (c) lineages that lacked tsung-hu were placed beneath lineages
with tsung-hu and categorized as "lower households"
(hsia-hu); and (d) the right of landownership was
guaranteed by the lineage organization.

Thus far I have introduced studies that have attempted structural comprehension of issues, and now
I shall examine this methodology. Three points can be
raised to describe it:

　　1. It stresses synchronic phenomena and explains mu-
　　　tual relationships. This is tantamount to saying we
　　　should rid ourselves of the analytic method, which
　　　detaches certain phenomena from the overall design
　　　and reduces the value of functionalism.

2. It explains things that give order to synchronic
   phenomena. For example, norm consciousness, custom,
   and world view that unconsciously prescribe human
   activity; market structure that prescribes economic
   activity and thought; ideas that support laws; and
   concepts that simultaneously exercise measured control over rulers and ruled as well as over rebels
   and suppressors of rebellion.[10]

3. By comparing two or more structures separated by
   space or time, it elucidates structural change and
   the unique characteristic of each structure. Note
   Takahashi's comparison of legal concepts for various
   eras and Kishimoto's comparison of two kinds of
   market areas, open and closed.

By emphasizing structure, it becomes possible to
deepen the confluence of social and cultural anthropology. At present, increased attention is being paid in
social anthropology to ethnic Han society, as in Segawa
Masahisa's "The Form of a Village: The Characteristics
of North Chinese Villages"[a] (Minzokugaku kenkyū 47.1).
It would seem necessary for Chinese historical research,
and by the same token social anthropology, to be concerned with the study of rural society in Hong Kong.

Social and Economic History
        Two essays take up the issue of landowning systems:
Fujii Hiroshi, "The Basic Structure of the One-Field
Two-Owners System (7)"[a] (Kindai Chūgoku 11); and Matsuda
Yoshirō, "On the Kuan-shih in Taiwan in the Ch'ing"[c]
(Chūgoku shi kenkyū, Ōsaka shiritsu daigaku 7). Fujii
continues his debate with Kusano Yasushi and, based on
archival material drawn from studies in China published
in recent years, he argues that it was in the early
Ch'ing that cultivation rights formed around "bonded
rent" (ya-tsu) in both Kwangtung and Kiangsi. Matsuda
clarifies the function of the kuan-shih, a personal

manager of sorts over reclaimant households, who with
official permission would bring together tenant farmers
to engage in land reclamation. As the controlling power
of the man in charge of land reclamation grew vis à vis
the tenants (because of the expansion of the one-field
two-owners system), the kuan-shih's management over the
village diminished and became a system of joint management by the property owners. We need to elucidate the
conceptual structure of land possession in the one-field
two-owners system, which supported the rights of both
landlords and tenants, not solely from the perspective
of its historical development.

Two studies examined taxation systems: Kawakatsu
Mamoru, "The Single Whip Reform in Wu-chin County,
Ch'ang-chou Prefecture, Nan-Chih-li (1)"[h] (Kyūshū daigaku
Tōyōshi ronshū 10); and Suzuki Hiroyuki, "The Development
of Tax Farming in the Ming Dynasty"[b] (Tōhōgaku 64).
Kawakatsu argues that the Single Whip reform, which represented the takeover of the tax system by the local
administration, was also a change pushed by various
localities themselves. He traces the actual process of
reform as it occurred in Wu-chin county. Suzuki claims
that as payment in silver for labor and expenses accompanying the transportation of goods advanced, it brought
on the development of pao-lan or tax farming. Pao-lan
by the local gentry and "clerks and runners" (hsü-li,
yamen underlings) appeared from the years of the Chia-
ching reign of the Ming.

In the area of water conservancy, Tani Mitsutaka
has written "River Conservancy Work in Hsü-chou and
Huai-an in the Transition from the Chia-ching to the
Wan-li Eras [of the Ming]"[a] (in Ono ronshū). Tani describes the deterioration, from the mid-Ming on, causing
breaches in embankments in the area of Hsü-chou and
Huai-an prefecture, which were due to changes in the
course of the main trunk of the Yellow River, and the

construction work done to handle these problems.

Three works dealt with issues of commerce, transportation, and cities: Shiba Yoshinobu, "Cities and Rural
Villages in Medieval and Early Modern China: A New Per-
spective on the Study of Urban History"[b] (Ōsaka daigaku
bungakubu kyōdō kenkyū ronshū 1); this volume was indi-
vidually entitled Kinsei toshi no hikaku shiteki kenkyū
(Comparative historical studies of early modern cities);
Morita Akira, "The Commercial Function of the Lu-kang
Garrison in Taiwan During the Ch'ing Dynasty"[g] (Tōyōshi
ron 4); and Hoshi Ayao's book, Dai'unga hatten shi:
Chōkō kara Kōga e (A history of the development of the
Grand Canal, from the Yangtze to the Yellow River).[d]

After explaining the theory of market areas, Shiba
argues the need for comparative studies of market structure. Morita describes the relationship between a migrant
populace and commercial routes by looking at the actual
movements of people in the wilds outside Lu-kang. Hoshi
translates extracts concerning grain transport and sea
transport from the Yüan-shih, Ming-shih, and Ch'ing-shih
kao, and he attaches commentary where necessary. Because
of its complete index, this book is extraordinarily useful.

Social history has come into its own in recent
years. Six essays in this field have been published:
Fuma Susumu, "A Short History of the T'ung-shan hui:
Toward an Understanding of the Late Ming and Early Ch'ing
in the History of Social Welfare in China"[d] (Shirin 65.4);
Kawakatsu Mamoru, "Thugs (ta-hang) and Vagrants (fang-
hsing) in the Late Ming and Early Ch'ing: Historical
Materials on Vagabonds in Pre-Modern Chinese Society"[i]
(Shien 109); Okuzaki Yūji, "Men Celebrated at the Hsiang-
hsien Shrine in Soochow Prefecture: On the Local Nature
of the Local Gentry"[c] (Mindaishi kenkyū 10); Okuzaki
Yūji, "The Descent Line of Gentry Family Wu of Wu-chiang
County, Soochow Prefecture"[d] (in Sakai ronshū); Shiroi
Takashi, "A Study of the Activities and Partisan Con-

flicts Among Local Sheng-yüan at the End of the Ming:
Concerning the Death by Flogging of a Chu-sheng by
Hsiung T'ing-pi, an Educational Inspector"[a] (Kyūshū
daigaku Tōyōshi ronshū 10).

Fuma explains the organization and ideology of the
movement of the T'ung-shan hui, and he describes how it
took embryonic form as a social gathering of literati.
He shows how, when transplanted to Kiangnan, it strength-
ened its nature as a welfare association and social
service organization. We need further analysis of its
relationship to the state's relief projects. Kawakatsu
is concerned with whether it is valid to limit popular
resistance of the early Ch'ing to men involved with
commerce, peasants, and bondservants. He attempts to
describe actual vagabonds (wu-lai) whose activities cannot be explained by class relations. Okuzaki's two
essays form the groundwork for a study of the gentry.

Political History

Danjō Hiroshi also tends toward structural understanding in his two essays: "The 'Virtuous' Mr. Cheng
and Late Yüan Society"[c] (Tōyō gakuhō 63.3-4); and "Ideal
and Reality in the Yüan-Ming Transition, with Reference
to the 'Virtuous' Mr. Cheng"[d] (Shirin 65.2). Danjō
grasps each of the following from a cultural perspective:
(a) Kiangnan society in the Yüan; (b) Kiangnan society
in the early Ming; and (c) a centralized, unified control. Thus, (a) had a degenerate structure because of
the fragility of Yüan control over Kiangnan and its
political alienation of Southern Chinese. Under such a
structure, rich men often engaged in activities of a
"profit-seeking sort" (rieki tsuikyū kei). As Yüan state
power weakened, activities of a "power-oriented sort"
(kenryoku shikō kei) also emerged. In (b) we witness
a structure that in the early Ming political system was
called the Southerners' regime. Here too we observe
activities of a "profit-seeking sort" wherein individuals

sought to expand their own interests by adhering to officials. While the Ming regime ruled North China, the base of
its existence remained in Kiangnan, and it sought to change
from this warped situation into a structure like (c).
The opportunity seized in cases such as Ming T'ai-tsu's
famous scandals[11] enabled the elimination of "profit-
seeking" wealthy men who represented an obstruction to
dynastic control, and also changed the bureaucratic
structure. Furthermore, in order to nurture wealthy men
concerned with "village maintenance" (kyōson iji kei),
which integrated with the structure of (c), the state
bestowed exaltation in the form of the appellation I-men
[upon select men] and established a school system. Then,
by moving the capital to Peking, a structure for (c) was
firmly in place. Danjō's second essay offers a bird's-
eye view of the diagram outlined above. His first essay
looks at the issue from the perspective of one rich individual concerned with "village maintenance." He points
out in comparing the three structures noted above that
(a) and (b) are continuous, while (b) and (c) enjoy
an intermittent relationship.

Inoue Hiromasa has written two essays: "The Opium
Issue in the Chia-ch'ing Period of the Ch'ing Dynasty:
Particularly on the Ban on Opium in the First Half of
the Chia-ch'ing Era"[a] (Shimane daigaku hōbungakubu kiyō
4.1); and "On the Opium Issue in the Chia-ch'ing and
Tao-kuang Eras of the Ch'ing Dynasty"[b] (Tōyōshi kenkyū
41.1). Inoue traces the policy changes concerning the
ban on opium from the Chia-ch'ing period, when the
issues (strictly speaking) first appeared until the
early Tao-kuang period just prior to the emergence of
the opium debate that was directly linked to the Opium
War. He pays special attention to the fact that in
order to protect themselves Kwangtung officials falsi-
fied intelligence reports to the central government.
This intelligence (including orders) was substantively

structured around institutions and the state apparatus.
One acutely senses the need for more research into the
mechanisms in China for the transfer of information.

Popular Rebellion

In his volume Sennen ōkoku teki minshū undō no
kenkyū: Chūgoku, Tōnan Ajia ni okeru (Studies of popular
millenarian movements in China and Southeast Asia),[c]
Suzuki Chūsei tends toward trying to explain in a unified pattern a large number of religious rebellions
that occurred in the Ming and Ch'ing.

Kobayashi Kazumi contributed an essay ("An Explanation of the White Lotus Rebellion of the Chia-ch'ing
Period"[e]) to the volume Chūgoku minshū hanran shi (vol.
3). He criticizes earlier periodization schemes for
rebellions, and he offers a periodization on the basis
of the ideology and organization of the White Lotus army.

In an article entitled "A Full Record of the Revolts
in Ssu-en and T'ien-chou[Kwangsi]: A Rebellion of Officials Sent to Rule Non-Chinese Tribes and Their Local
Chiefs in the Yu River Valley of Kwangsi in the Mid-
Ming and the Policy of Transferring Authority over Tribes-
people from the Local Chiefs to Regular Officials"[a]
(Shien, Rikkyō daigaku shigakkai 42.1-2), Taniguchi
Fusao deals with the relationship between the government
policy of using delegated officials to take away control
exercised by local chieftains over their tribesmen and
the upper stratum of the minority peoples.

Finally, Kurita Satoru's essay "On the T'ien-li-
chiao Rebellion"[a] (Shien, Rikkyō daigaku shigakkai 42.2)
attempts to explain the origins of the T'ien-li-chiao.

Thought and Culture

In his essay "Management by 'Owner Farmers' in the
Yangtze Delta in the Late Ming and Early Ch'ing: The
Principle of Self-Cultivation for Gentleman-Farmer Chang
Lü-hsiang"[d] (Tochi seido shigaku 96), Iwama Kazuo

analyzes Chang's thought and his work <u>Pu nung-shu</u>
(Supplementary agricultural handbook).[12]   Iwama finds
here that commodity production was based on privilege.

A welcome event indeed is the appearance of a
translation of the writings of Matteo Ricci by Kawana
Kōhei under the title <u>Chūgoku Kirisuto kyō fukyō shi (1)</u>
(A history of Christian missionary work in China).[a]   An
explanation of Chinese realities at the time and of
Ricci's influence on China would make happy additions.

I have in this essay been less concerned with
development than I have with emphasizing the emergence
of a trend toward structural understanding. There are
people who will be apprehensive in the face of such a
trend, for the abandonment of a theory of developmental
stages, they may feel, will bring about a new "theory
of stagnation." However, to the extent that structural
understanding is a methodology in search of a specific
historical reality in China, this is a needless anxiety.
We must not forget that a theory of developmental
stages linked to modernization theory proved powerless
when the inclination toward a new colonialism reared
its head in Japanese confrontations with Asia.

JAPANESE STUDIES OF POST-OPIUM WAR CHINA: 1982

Satō Kimihiko, in
Shigaku zasshi 92.5
(May 1983), 199-207.

As one Japanese scholar of the modern and contemporary history of China, I feel the most important event that must first be raised as we look back over the year 1982 is the "textbook issue," which erupted in the summer and spawned wide repercussions. Both the fact that the problem started as criticism and external pressure from a major power (China) and the fact that fervent arguments in the press were finally resolved through diplomacy were extremely Japanese ways of generating and then coping with a problem. The fact that the numerous views that arose branched out in many directions demonstrates that the scope of this issue was not confined merely to the accounts in the new history texts. The criticism from the peoples of Asia severely questioned how our postwar Japanese society regarded its responsibilities toward Asia, and in the final analysis the debate has much significance for the very national mentality of Japanese society.

In the area of historiography, what postwar historical research and historical education have achieved is one of the things brought into question. Although the problem may be seen as a conflict between progressive authors of textbooks and progressive historians on the one hand, and the Ministry of Education on the other, I believe it to be a more basic rivalry between a postwar historiography and historical education based on reason and the institution of the Ministry of Education, which

typifies the national mentality of Japanese society.
Thus, despite all the ties forged not by the academic
community but by Japanese society and the Japanese mentality to the nations of Asia, the severe criticisms
from the peoples of Asia and the Ministry's response to
it must call into question historical research and
historical education in Japan.

I myself have reflected long and hard on the in-
completeness of our knowledge of Asia as well as on the
powerlessness of any single educator. Just as our
national character warms up as easily as it cools down,
domestic concern for our neighboring countries in this
textbook affair seems now to have settled down and the
arguments have apparently been calmed. Despite the
tumult that has ensued, if the present state of Japanese
society is such that the matter can only be settled in
this way, we cannot forget the severity with which our
Asian neighbors have looked upon us. How do we deal
with this issue? How are we to confer substance on it?
These are major tasks that remain for scholars of modern
and contemporary Asian history as well as of Japanese
history and for historical educators. Insofar as this
is an issue deeply linked with the nature of Japanese
society since the Meiji period, it will surely resurface
again under a changed guise. Rather than forget what
transpired in 1982, I want to make it a lesson for the
future.

Turning our attention to the past year's research,
one notes the striking abundance of materials important
for studying the modern and contemporary eras in Chinese
history. Last year saw the publication of numerous
scholarly works. Banno Ryōkichi has put together a
summary analysis of scholarly trends in China in his
essay "New Developments in Modern and Contemporary
Scholarly Research Since the Cultural Revolution"[c] (in
Chūgoku rekishi gakkai no shin dōkō: Shin sekki kara

gendai made [New trends in Chinese historical scholarship, from neolithic to contemporary times]). Although
in Japan we are sometimes compelled to criticize the
atomized, scattered state of research, this is a virtual necessity in the great transitional era in which
Japanese scholarship on modern and contemporary China
now finds itself, as many scholars would agree. For
awhile, I think, we shall be consuming the wealth of
historical materials and delving deeply into concrete
problems, while various and sundry groping efforts will
continue to come forward in our respective areas of
expertise. Although many opinions different from my
own may be offered, I should like to treat the studies
mentioned below by historical eras.

The Taiping Rebellion

We have the following five essays concerned with
the Taipings: (1) Morita Akira, "Native-Hakka Feuds in
Kwangtung and the Local Power Structure in the Ch'ing:
The Case of Ling-hsi"[h] (in Kenryoku kōzō); (2) Nakayama
Yoshihiro, "The Power Structure of the Taiping Heavenly
Kingdom"[b] (in Kenryoku kōzō); (3) Kojima Shinji, "The
Depositions of Ten Taiping Soldiers from the Early
Period, Held in the Public Record Office of London"[c]
(Rekishi to bunka, Tōkyō daigaku kyōyōbu 14); (4) Takeuchi
Fusashi, "On the Miao Rebellion of the Taiping Years:
Centering on the Miao Region in Southern Kweichow"[a]
(Shichō N.S. 12); and (5) Namiki Yorihisa, "The Rent
Resistance Rebellion of the Lien-chuang hui in Honan in
the 1850's"[d] (Chūgoku kindaishi kenkyū 2).

Morita argues that the social upheavals after the
Opium War intensified class contradictions. As the
anti-Ch'ing movement of impoverished native (punti) and
Hakka peasants and the activities of native bandits commenced, both native bandits and gentry stirred up an
anti-Hakka consciousness among the native populace

and induced large-scale conflict between natives and
Hakkas. Morita mentions cases in which officials also
strove to conspire with the native people, and he suggests the position in which Hakka family members may
have found themselves at that time.

Nakayama claims that the basic power structure of
the Taiping Heavenly Kingdom was the "communitarian"
society of one large family, and he argues that it
deteriorated from a peasant to a landlord regime. The
conception of the "communitarian" society of one large
family is closely tied to the issue recently raised by
Wang Ch'ing-ch'eng in his essay "The 'Large Family' and
the 'Small Family' of the Taipings' Shang-ti"[a] (Li-shih
yen-chiu 1982, number 6), and it deserves further work.

Kojima introduces and analyzes the original texts
of ten extremely interesting depositions given by low-
level soldiers of the Taiping Army. Among the views he
presents are the following: (a) part of the main reason
these men accepted the God-Worshipping faith was the
promise of benefits in this world; (b) the theory of
the Taipings' 1851/1/11 raising of troops has to be
revised, and their troop levels in the early period
were around 20,000; (c) it seems that polygamy emerged
as a means for the leadership, from Hung Hsiu-ch'uan on
down, to display its authority and power; (d) the
Taipings permitted the existence of the King of Celestial
Virtue as a symbol to integrate new members originally
from the Heaven and Earth Society, and later when this
secret society was broken up and reorganized.

Takeuchi shows that earlier Japanese studies of
this Miao uprising demonstrated a process of impoverishment in Miao society at the time. He shows that at the
root of this rebellion, which began in opposition to the
enforcement of land tax exactments for raising money to
suppress the Taipings, lay a bond between the autonomous, communal character of Miao society as represented

by the organization of i-lang -- an autonomous, unified
organization of solidarity in the fortified villages --
and the outlaw activities of so-called "Miao bandits."
This study is noteworthy as a new trend toward pioneer-
ing in previously uncharted terrain.

Namiki analyzes the variegated economic background
that caused the Lien-chuang hui, a rural self-defense
organization formed to fight off the Taipings' northern
expedition, to give rise to frequent anti-official and
rent resistance riots. He argues that because of the
economic chaos accompanying a fluctuation in the relative
value of silver coinage and newly issued paper currency,
the trade value assigned to transport grain and the
assessment of river conservancy materials were together
with the land tax levy for peasant farmers unfair and
excessive burdens. Namiki demonstrates that the Lien-
chuang hui was one part of a nationwide rent resistance
struggle at the time. Although there is an important
issue in the "jump" this struggle made as it transcended
the confines of a struggle to improve conditions and
exhibited its distinctive development into an uprising,
Namiki reserves this problem for his subsequent research.

Early Westernization and the 1898 Reform Periods

Sōda Saburō, in his essay "Cocoon Transactions in
the Kiangsu-Chekiang Region"[e] (Shigaku kenkyū 156),
centers his analysis on the institution of cocoon firms
through which gentry in cocoon-producing areas such as
Wu-hsi managed the structure of raw cocoon transactions
and which was an important aspect of the formation of a
modern silk industry centered on Shanghai. This essay
forms one part of Sōda's research on the silk industry,
and the whole work deserves a separate evaluation.

In his essay "Ch'ing-liu in Late Ch'ing China and
the Activities of Entrepreneurs: The Career and Role of
Chang Chien"[c] (in Nitchū kankei to bunka masatsu),

Nakai Hideki diligently traces the life history of
literatus Chang Chien as an "entrepreneur" who shouldered China's early industrialization amidst a value
system and social order severely shaken. He looks at
Chang's activities in relation to his ethics and the
"business climate" surrounding him. Although his
ch'ing-liu (puritanical literati) disposition contributed, Nakai notes, to certain successes as an entrepreneur, Chang Chien the entrepreneur tried to make up
for the lack of conditions appropriate to the embourgeoisement of Chinese society -- namely, the "business
climate" for capitalism -- and for that reason had to
become involved in politics (the constitutionalist movement). One of the major accomplishments of this study
is Nakai's elucidation of the nature of the political
group known as the Ch'ing-liu-p'ai and the personal
qualities of the men in it in the politics of the late
Ch'ing dynasty. However, this excellent work also
presents a fresh investigation of the embourgeoisement
of Chinese society from a perspective that goes beyond
the framework of economic history.

In the same volume we find an essay by Yang T'ien-
i, "The Rivalry Between Native Spinning and the Japanese
Spinning Industry in China."[a] Yang outlines the causes
behind and the forms taken by the Japanese spinning industry in the early history of its advance into China
with an eye to its rivalry with the native Chinese
spinning industry. He then compares and analyzes the
management of native spinning and Japanese spinning in
China. He argues that one thing that made it hard to
manage native spinning was the phenomenon of "valuing
cotton and disparaging gauze" (mien-kuei sha-chien)
caused by the organization of trade along the divergent
and manifold routes of the Chinese marketing system.
Yet, despite the pre-modern nature of the Chinese marketing system, the Japanese spinning industry in China

attained a superior position in the Chinese markets in
the 1920's and 1930's by confronting this problem with
an organized and aggressive behavioral pattern of
building structures to buy and sell directly [without
recourse to Chinese middlemen--JAF]. After a time it
put pressure on native spinning and drove it to bankruptcy. This behavioral pattern of the Japanese spinning industry in China, he notes, is no different from
our postwar present one: "Japanese business is completely
callous in its negative influence and oppressive function through various spots in Asia," and the conflict
between the peoples of Asia "has been exacerbated by
Japanese misunderstandings."

Kishimoto Mio's essay "The Place in the History of
Economic Thought of the Idea of Markets in Tsu-ho"[d]
(Chūgoku kindaishi kenkyū 2) describes how the notion
of "cultivating the basis" (p'ei-pen) in T'ao Hsü's
essay Tsu-ho dealt with the issue of working people as
consumers and is novel in this regard in the history
of Chinese economic thought.

Ōno Santoku has written "The Development of National Capitalist Industry in Shanghai and Its Characteristics: The Case of the Nanyang Brothers Tobacco Company"[a]
(Kōchi kōgyō kōtō senmon gakkō gakujutsu kiyō 18). He
looks at the period from the creation of the Nanyang
Brothers establishment through the 1920's in its
rivalries with the British-American Tobacco Company.
When he examines the nature of this domestic industrial
enterprise, he notes its links with overseas Chinese
for capital as well as business, and we see management
participation through a board of directors of brokers
and bank authorities -- indicating a highly complex
structure. Thus, this overall study of the history of
the Nanyang Brothers enterprise demonstrates that its
development was impeded by attacks from "British-
American Tobacco" and by the heavy taxation and surtaxes

of the government. We need more and more studies like
this one in the future.

Murai Tomohide's essay, "Expansionism and the
Military in 19th Century China"[a] (Gunji shigaku 17.4),
offers a critical perspective on the accepted theory
that the formation of Sinkiang province in Eastern
Turkestan was aimed at colonization and set the stage
for the absorption of various contradictions in (Han)
Chinese society after the pacification of the Taipings.
However, he consistently pursues a simple argument,
explaining that military activities carried out under
the leadership of Tso Tsung-t'ang developed directly
from the social problems in Hunan accompanying the dis-
banding of the Hunan Army. Clearly, Han Chinese colonial activities did in fact take place, but, as the
military is the concentrated manifestation of politics,
it is rather hasty to argue "expansionism" without an
investigation of the debates on sea and border defenses
that ensued in the process of policy determination as
the Ch'ing responded to Russian and English moves in
the Northeast.

We also have Kataoka Kazutada's article, "The
Ko-lao-hui in Sinkiang"[c] (in Sakai ronshū). He argues
that the Ko-lao-hui organization, which grew inside the
Hunan Army (responsible for military activities [in
Sinkiang--JAF]), spread as a mutual aid association of
Han Chinese who migrated to Sinkiang after the establishment of provincial government. Then it linked up with
the local Moslem populace, and at the time of the 1911
Revolution made contact with the revolutionaries. He
shows how after the Revolution under the administration
of Yang Tseng-hsin it was suppressed and eventually
fell apart.

Shirai Takeko's essay "Braves in the Era of the
Nien Rebellion: The Nien Uprising and Han Chinese
Officials"[a] (Shien, Rikkyō daigaku shigakkai 41.2)

offers a relatively complete overview of the goals and
actions of the Nien rebels. She looks at the process
through which the Ch'ing dynasty's main fighting force
changed from Senggerinchin's Mongol army to Tseng Kuo-
fan's Hunan Army to the Huai Army of Li Hung-chang in
the course of fighting with the Nien.

Sasaki Masaya has begun an essay entitled "A Study
of the Anti-Foreign Movement in the Late Ch'ing (1)"[b]
(Kindai Chūgoku 12). In response to the British policy
seeking to open a port at Ch'ao-chou as stipulated under the Treaty of Tientsin, the "anti-British struggle
of Ch'ao-chou gentry and local people" -- through a ten-
year period resistance by the inhabitants who were fear-
ful of the economic dislocations a port opening would
cause -- was primarily caused by the fragile control of
the Ch'ing local authorities over the local populace.
This struggle also demonstrated the uncompromising
resistance of the semi-autonomous surrounding villages.
Sasaki shows that the rioters were routed by the
British forces and effective control in the villages
was established together with local officials. He argues that we can thus really understand the forging of
a cooperative organization -- the strengthening of support for the Ch'ing government as rulers over the
people who were opposed to the English intrusion. Furthermore, although he explains the concrete process of
the various cases involving Christian missionaries
(chiao-an) in Kweichow, Nan-ch'ang, Hsiang-t'an, Heng-
chou, and Hsi-yang in the T'ung-chih reign, he makes
extremely interesting observations about how the intensified activities of the Christian church appeared to
Chinese gentry and peasants in these places after the
Taiping Rebellion. This work is likely to become one
of basic importance. Sasaki has also published a segment of a work in progress entitled "A Study of the
Opium War"[a] (Kindai Chūgoku 11).

The Boxer Movement

The journal _Shichō_ (N.S. 11) ran a special issue
on the Boxers which included the following articles:
Sun Tso-min, "Chinese Studies of the Boxer Movement"[a];
Joseph W. Esherick, "Missionaries, Chinese Church Mem-
bers, and the Boxers: Imperialism in the Guise of
Christianity"[a]; Satō Kimihiko, "Various Images of the
Boxer Movement in Its Early Years: The Large Sword
Society and Church Activities"[c]; Kuroha Kiyotaka,
"Japanese Views of the 'Boxer Bandits': An Aspect of
the History of the Boxer Movement from Japanese Histori-
cal Materials"[a]; and an essay by Saitō Seki on the re-
sponse of the European socialists, primarily the German
Socialist Party, at the time of the Boxer Incident.

Sun's essay, on the basis of a survey of Chinese
studies of the Boxers, criticizes the method of evaluation employed by Wang Chih-chung in his article "Feudal
Ignorance and the Boxer Movement."[a] Sun argues against
Wang's view that the theoretical structure of the
Boxers was incapable of resistance to colonialism and
that this ideological weakness was detrimental in
practice as well.

Esherick notes that subjectively the Boxer masses
rose up in opposition to a foreign religion and that it
is important to focus on the activities of foreign
missionaries and Chinese converts. He plunges into
this issue by making use of the voluminous documents of
the missionaries held in America. He argues that in the
1890's in Europe and America a fierce enthusiam to con-
vert the world to Christianity emerged and eventually
joined together with imperialist policies. The Sheng-
yen hui, which furthered missionary work in Shantung,
symbolized this movement in actual practice. The
Catholic Church, which held China in utter contempt,
formed a hierarchy with its pinnacle at the embassies
in Peking in a rivalry with the Chinese bureaucracy.

The missionaries thus constituted a politically coer-
cive force in the eyes of the Chinese. Esherick argues
that if the church and the missionaries were seen as
political entities, a contradictory understanding about
Christianity itself became possible. Thus, he sees the
aggression of Christianity, backed up by imperialist
troops particularly after the Germans turned Tsingtao
into a base, as a situation similar to Vietnam at the
time of the Sino-French War when missionaries served as
the advance guard for imperialist encroachment. Under
these circumstances the anti-Christian organization
played a patriotic, anti-imperialist role, he argues,
and he evaluates their resistance quite positively.

In an essay entitled "The Origins of the Boxers:
The Eight Trigrams Sect and the Boxers"[d] (Shigaku
zasshi 91.1), Satō Kimihiko argues that the Boxers, who
were religiously connected to the Ch'ing-shui sect of
Wang Lun in the Ch'ien-lung era, appeared in the T'ien-
li-chiao Rebellion of the Chia-ch'ing era. The martial
arts of boxing and fencing in which they were influenced
by the Eight Trigrams sect continued later in the rural
areas of western Shantung. By virtue of the Boxers'
adherence to martial arts, Satō locates their origin in
the martial wing of the Eight Trigrams. In his article
on the early Boxer movement cited above, Satō points
out that in the critical situation for peasant society
in western Shantung after the Sino-Japanese War, the
Large Sword Society was formed as a rural self-protec-
tive association solidified around the martial art of
"imperviousness to swords and spears." This was the
point of departure for what would later develop into
the Boxers.

Kuroha, as scholar of Japan's fifteen-year war
with China, argues that despite the fact that the Japanese
had valuable observations and experience with respect
to the Boxers, they only took from that a negative, even

belittling, evaluation of popular Chinese nationalism.
Thirty years later the Japanese Army once again met the
popular resistance of the descendants of the Large
Sword Society and the Red Spears. He sees here the
historical place of a distinctly Japanese "Boxer"
experience and sharply notes that those men in charge
of the military diplomacy of the Japanese Empire did
not learn from this significant repetition of history.

Kobayashi Kazumi has also written on this subject:
"The Boxer Movement, Thought and Religion"[f] (in I-ho-
t'uan yün-tung shih t'ao-lun wen-chi [Collection of
essays from the Symposium on the History of the Boxer
Movement]). He takes the view that attention should be
directed toward the unemployed, "non-permanent residents
outside the villages" in the Boxer movement.

The 1911 Revolution and the Early Republic

Three articles that reported on the Scholarly
Symposium Commemorating the Seventieth Anniversary of
the 1911 Revolution (held in Wuhan in October 1982)
were Nozawa Yutaka, "The Seventieth Anniversary of the
1911 Revolution and Studies of Modern and Contemporary
Chinese History"[e] (Rekishi hyōron 386); Ishida Yoneko's
essay for Chūgoku kenkyū geppō (#409), which introduces
some materials and offers her impressions of the conference; and Kubota Bunji, "Notes on a Trip to the
Seventieth Anniversary [Conference] on the 1911 Revolution"[d] (Shisō* 23). Nozawa introduces the numerous
papers introduced at the conference and clarifies the
major arguments. He offers as well the prediction that
in the future Chinese studies of the 1911 Revolution
will accord it a place of great importance as an epochal
event.

Hazama Naoki, who was present at the symposium,
has written "Class Conflict in the Era of the 1911
Revolution"[d] (Chūgoku kenkyū geppō 409). Because of

the formation of more national economic structures in
the Ch'ing, a Chinese bourgeoisie found a place in the
middle ground of fundamentally opposed structures --
between the exactions of imperialist and feudal rulers
and the peasant class. This essay makes a determined
effort to explain this arrangement of classes.

Because of the limitations imposed by incomplete
statistics, must we often be sadly resigned to having
to use hypothetical numbers? Kuroda Akinobu considers
problems relating to this issue in his excellent essay,
"Monetary Reforms in Hupeh Province During the Late
Ch'ing: Provincial Power as an Economic Structure"[a]
(Tōyōshi kenkyū 41.3). The monetary reforms of Chang
Chih-tung concerning the official treasuries (kuan-
ch'ien-chü) emerged because, although their direct impetus was to acquire profits from minting to compensate
for deficiencies in state finances, in essence their
subsumption into world markets necessitated reform of
the structure of currency circulation. Because official
treasuries functioned as organs to extend credit and
because bills of value replaced hard currencies (silver
coinage) as a means of general circulation of copper
coins (t'ung-yüan, equal to ten pieces of copper cash)
and official notes (kuan-ch'ien-p'iao, exchangeable
paper currency), these currencies functioned as a means
of purchasing agricultural goods, and they linked the
peasant economy to the treaty port economy. This
development prepared the conditions for the accumulation of commercial capital, and provincial power as an
"economic structure" became a mechanism of its promotion, according to Kuroda. They shed light on the
phenomenon of independence in the trend to provincial
separation as the unit of commercial capital accumulation in the late Ch'ing.

Ishida Yoneko presented a paper at the conference
entitled "On Peasant Struggles and the Role of the

Kuang-fu hui in Chekiang During the Ch'ing"[c] (Chūgoku
kenkyū geppō 409). She argues that the religious antag-
onisms of entire villages under the leadership of the
landlord-gentry class, which had a mass base in the
period of the Boxer Rebellion, was continued into the
revolutionary movement through the efforts of the
Kuang-fu hui to direct the secret society leaders
(active in these religious struggles) toward revolution.
Their bond with peasant struggles, however, was only
indirect, for after the frustrations of the Kuang-fu
hui in 1907 the landlord-gentry had to respond to and
overcome the new high tide of peasant uprisings
against the new government. Ishida offers an overall
perspective on their historical role.

      Kusunose Masaaki in his essay "On the Nanking
Provisional Government"[c] (in Kenryoku kōzō) criticizes
the view that sees the Provisional Government as either
an allied regime of members of the T'ung-meng hui, the
constitutional reformers, and the old bureaucrats, or
as a revolutionary regime under T'ung-meng hui control.
He sees its role lying in the extent to which, under
the initiative of Sun Yat-sen and the T'ung-meng hui
who held real power in the government, they could
compel the Ch'ing emperor to abdicate, establish a
republican form of government, and bring about the
presidency of Yüan Shih-k'ai by peacefully negotiating
in joint meetings with the representatives of the
various provincial authorities under the leadership
of the constitutionalists. The Provisional Government,
he argues, eventually succeeded despite making great
concessions.

      In his essay "On the Chinese National Assembly"[d]
(Shingai kakumei kenkyū 2), Kojima Yoshio argues that
the Chinese National Assembly in Japan, where it was
formed by the T'ung-meng hui leaders after the experience of the Canton uprising, was created as an auxiliary

organization of the T'ung-meng hui to advance the revolutionary movement by stimulating Chinese students in
Japan.

We also have a volume by Kamikōchi Ken'ichi,
Nihon ryūgaku to kakumei undō (Overseas studies in
Japan and the revolutionary movement).[a] It was published
as one in the series on comparative cultures, but deserves further review.

The May Fourth Era

Ōhata Tokushirō, in his article "The 1911 Revolution and Japan's Response" (Nihon rekishi 414), claims
that Japan's basic response, be it an aggressive call
for the independence (i.e., partition) of Manchuria and
Mongolia or for a peaceful accommodation with the government, was to protect and preserve its interests in
Southern Manchuria and Eastern Mongolia as well as to
attempt to cultivate influence (i.e., advance its
interests) in China proper. Ōhata thinks that the
advocacy of and tendency toward the expansion of
Japanese interests in China at this time was connected
in certain respects to the formation of the Twenty-One
Demands.

This issue is dealt with by Fujimoto Hiroo in his
essay "Japanese Imperialism and the May Fourth Movement"[a]
(in Goshi undō no kenkyū). Fujimoto locates in the
cabinet meetings (under the second Katsura Cabinet) of
August 25, 1908, the beginnings of a diplomatic direction
toward China that led to the formation of the Twenty-
One Demands. He claims that the modern bureaucrats of
the Foreign Ministry controlled policy concerning China
at that time. He demonstrates that their policy called
for an invasion of economic privilege [vis à vis China]
and was a quintessentially modern, imperialist policy.
He shows, however, that they pushed for this policy
with the possibility and preparation of a military invasion lurking in the background. Thus, while the

anti-Japanese movement was "radicalized" during the
May Fourth Movement, the terror inspired by the "radicals"
forced reconciliation between the two kinds of imperial-
ists in Japan. Fujimoto details how this gave birth
to a shift under the Hara Cabinet toward a policy to
suppress the movement.

Volume One of Goshi undō no kenkyū was one of the
great pieces of work from the past year. In addition
to Fujimoto's essay, two others should be noted.
Hazama Naoki's "Introduction to Research on the May
Fourth Movement: The Role of the Proletariat in the
May Fourth Movement"[e] argues that the role played in
the Movement by the "three strikes"[1] of the working
class in Shanghai after June 8, that is to say the
"leadership" of the proletariat, gave a new quality to
the May Fourth Movement. Also, Kataoka Kazutada's essay
"A Short History of the May Fourth Movement in Tientsin"[d]
centers on the movement to boycott Japanese goods. It
traces the struggles from the inception of the May
Fourth Movement (on May 5) in Tientsin, noted for
being the base of Japanese commercial activities in
North China, through the collapse of the fight with its
suppression in January 1920. This volume on the May
Fourth Movement is worthy of a detailed critique by a
well-qualified scholar, so I shall not continue with it
here except to say that the viewpoint expressed in
Hazama's article might be placed on the agenda for
debate.

Intellectual History

One important achievement in the area of intellectual history is Maruyama Matsuyuki's volume Chūgoku
kindai no kakumei shisō (Revolutionary thought in modern
China),[b] although it deserves a review all its own.

Satō Yutaka has written "The Principle of 'National
Essence' (Kuo-ts'ui) and the Formation of 'National

Learning' (Kuo-hsüeh) in the journal Kuo-ts'ui hsüeh-
pao"[a] (Nihon Chūgoku gakkaihō 34). Satō investigates
the group of men who published the journal Kuo-ts'ui
hsüeh-pao. Their aim was to foster a sense of sorrowful
parting with the Han people's cultural and spiritual
inheritance -- namely, kuo-ts'ui or national essence --
and to raise Han racial consciousness through the reinvestigation of Chinese civilization at a time of
shifting world views caused by the Western impact. They
advocated "national learning" (including the non-canonical
philosophers of antiquity and other schools of the Chou
and Ch'in periods), which was a search for the "national
essence" quite distinct from traditional scholarship
(Confucianism) since the Ch'in and Han. They were intent on reviving ancient civilization. Gradually, though,
Satō notes, they tended to become engrossed in antiquari-
anism and lost their radical, innovative edge. Their
efforts were continued in the new era following the
1911 Revolution and set the basis for making new
explorations later.

Gotō Nobuko has written an article with a wealth
of information, "The Emergence of Yün Tai-ying: Thought
on the Eve of the May Fourth Period"[c] (Shinshū daigaku
jimbun kagaku ronshū 16). She argues that the career
of Yün Tai-ying, a central leader of the Wuchang Mutual
Aid Society who devoted himself to this organization
around the time of the May Fourth Movement, can be
divided into three parts: (a) just prior to the May
Fourth Movement, (b) 1918 to the summer of 1922, and
(3) after his entrance into the Chinese Communist Party.
In a penetrating analysis of the first period, Gotō
looks at how Yün absorbed the anarchism of Kropotkin
and sought to build a new philosophy of life and
morality. She also examines the uniqueness of his view
of knowledge and his mode of thinking, which served as
the basis for a critique of feudal customs, religion,

and beliefs; thus, the view of an ideal society that he was in the midst of forming. From this analysis, she concludes that the activities of the Wuchang Mutual Aid Society -- "an organization for self-improvement and for public service on behalf of society" -- point to the intellectual destination Yün was groping toward in this period.

One further essay that raises important issues is Katayama Tsuyoshi, "The T'u-chiao-piao and Problems Surrounding It for the Pearl River Delta of Kwangtung in the Late Ch'ing: Land Taxes, Household Registers, and Lineage"[a] (Shigaku zasshi 91.4). Looking at the T'u-chia-piao, which was transcribed into local gazetteers of the Pearl River delta for the Late Ch'ing and Republican era, he argues against the commonly held theory that the li-chia system had fallen apart roughly at the same time that the ti-ting-yin (land-and-head tax) system was implemented at the start of the 18th century. He notes that through the late Ch'ing the t'u-chia (equivalent to li-chia) system continued to exist in the Pearl River delta. Also, the tax-paying households at whatever level in the t'u-chia system[2] who were responsible for tax collection on the official registers were probably not the individual residential family units. It is hoped that Katayama will continue his research in this area further.

Popular Movements and the History of the People[3]

We have three articles in this area of research: Noguchi Tetsurō, "The Red, White, and Yellow Sects in Kiangsi at the End of the Ch'ing"[d] (in Sakai ronshū); Suzuki Tomoo, "On Tea Houses in Kiangsu and Chekiang in the Late Ch'ing"[d] (in Sakai ronshū); and Watanabe Atsushi, "The Activities of the Green Gang and Bands of Salt Smugglers in the Lower Yangtze Delta at the End of the Ch'ing: A Look at Contacts in the Trafficking of

Smuggled Salt"[e] (in <u>Sakai ronshū</u>).

Noguchi examines the Red, White, and Yellow Sects
(three parts of a single religious society) in Southern
Kiangsi during the T'ung-chih period. He sees the Yellow Sect (similar to the Green Lotus of the Lo Sect)
and the Red Lotus (directly linked to the Red Lotus
Sect) forming constituent elements of currents in the
Lantern Flower Sect of Liu I-shun, who drew on the
"white line" pedigree of the White Lotus Sect of the
Chia-ch'ing period. We can also see here, he argues,
shadows cast by the smoldering embers of the Taipings
(i.e., the "religion of Hung Hsiu-ch'uan"), the Miao
people, and the Ko-lao-hui. This essay shows that we
should consider relations with the Taipings in our view
of the religious societies of South China in the late
Ch'ing. It is my feeling that there is a basic current,
including the Lantern Flower Sect, from the Lo Sect to
the Green Lotus Sect (Golden Elixir Path Sect) to the
Red, White, and Yellow Sects, the Great Way of Former
Heaven, and the Fellowship of Goodness Society. Furthermore, it is essential to note that the term <u>pai-
lien-chiao</u> served as a general noun indicating popular
secret religions generally during the Ming-Ch'ing period.

Suzuki's article is an enchantingly interesting
social history depicting various aspects of tea houses
in the people's social lives: as a club, meeting place,
court of law, theater, story-telling place, gambling
parlor, and opium den, a place where low-lifes and
secret societies came together.

Watanabe explains the traffic in smuggled salt in
the lower Yangtze delta and the Kiangsu-Chekiang region
from the Tao-kuang through the T'ung-chih into the mid-
Kuang-hsü reigns. Using a formidable amount of source
materials, he traces the relations and contacts of the
Green Gang and other salt-smuggling groups closely tied
to this region.

In the same volume in which these three essays
appear are three others that space allows me only to
mention: Taga Akigorō, "On Rules for Charitable Estates
During the Heyday of the Clans"[a]; Imahori Seiji, "Documents on the Slave Trade in the Republican Period and
the Family System"[b]; and Fukuzawa Hideo, "The 1898
Reform Movement and the Modern-Style Schools."[d]

Finally, I have a request for you all. A man of
shallow learning like myself honestly becomes exhausted
reading essays in Japanese that quote classical Chinese
texts in Chinese, and I am often tempted to dispense
with the whole effort mid-way. Perhaps, lacking
knowledge and training, I am alone in feeling this way,
but I would hope that in the future you will translate
quoted sources into Japanese in your essays.

NOTES

(All notes are the translator's unless otherwise noted)

Chapter 1.

1. <u>Mai-chia</u> refers to the subsoil rights which remained in the hands of the landlord; the landlord had the
right to levy a land rent from his tenant because he
(the landlord) had supposedly paid out several years'
land tax in advance. <u>Ch'eng-chia</u> refers to the topsoil;
the landlord conferred upon the tenant the capacity to
till the land with the understanding that the tenant would
repay the advance payment already made by the landlord.
<u>Mai-chia</u> and <u>ch'eng-chia</u> are intimately connected and
both are linked to the one-field two-owners system. See
Hoshi Ayao, <u>Chūgoku shakai keizai goi</u>[a](hereafter, Hoshi),
pp. 345, 196.

2. <u>Kuo-t'ou</u>: payment to the landlord of a specified
amount per 1000 <u>pu</u> of embankment when they were completed.
See Hoshi, p. 37. Each <u>pu</u> equals 1.60 meters. The best
secondary discussion of these systems remains Niida
Noboru, <u>Chūgoku hōsei shi kenkyū, tochihō torihiki hō</u>[a],
pp. 183-85.

3. "Gentry control" (<u>kyōshin shihai</u>) and "theories
of the gentry" (<u>kyōshin ron</u>) have been the topics of debate in Japanese sinology for some time. A good introduction to the historiography of these debates is Mori
Masao's three-part essay, "Theories of the Gentry in
Japanese Ming-Ch'ing Historical Studies"[a] (<u>Rekishi
hyōron</u> 308 (Dec. 1975), pp. 40-60; 312 (Apr. 1976),
pp. 74-84; 314 (June 1976), pp. 113-28).

4. <u>Ch'i-chuang-hu</u>: rich households which would buy
lands in other districts so as to avoid local <u>corvée</u>
requirements. See Hoshi, p. 71.

5. See Mori Masao, "Notes on the Landlord System
in Che-hsi in the Latter Half of the Fourteenth Century."[b]

6. This point contradicts Ray Huang's assertion that
it began in 1436. See Taxation and Government Finance
in Sixteenth Century Ming China, p. 52.

7. Che-liang-yin: commuted tax, i.e., from grain to
silver. See Hoshi, p. 240; and Hoshi Ayao, Chūgoku
shakai keizai goi zokuhen (hereafter, Hoshi, zokuhen),
p. 45. The latter contradicts Hoshi's earlier (p. 88)
appraisal that the two were substantively the same.

8. Shun-chuang-fa: a Ch'ing system of dividing
rural villages. See Hoshi, zokuhen, p. 87.

9. The nu in nu-pien comes from nu-p'u who were not
slaves but bondservants. There were many levels of
nu-p'u which makes translation of the term difficult.
See Joseph P. McDermott, "Bondservants in the T'ai-hu
Basin During the Late Ming: A Case of Mistaken Iden-
tities," Journal of Asian Studies XL.4 (Aug. 1981),
pp. 675-701.

Chapter 2.

1. For more information about "theories of the
gentry" and "gentry control," see p. 176, n. 3 above.

2. See Mizoguchi, "The Thought of the Tung-lin
Faction,"[a] discussed above pp. 20-21.

3. See Hoshi, p. 57.

4. See above p. 8.

Chapter 3

1. See Hoshi, p. 117. Ku are comparable to modern-
day stocks or shares.

2. Coolies or other impoverished peasants who
sought refuge in Kwangtung ports after the Opium War
were often seized and put into virtual slavery overseas.

They were known as chu-tzu, the "pig" (chu) element deriving from a derogatory reference to the queue. Poor
women (prostitutes, opium den women, and other social
low-life) were often sold into slavery in Kwangtung to
serve as prostitutes overseas in Europe and America.
The "flower" element or hua in the Cantonese carries
the implication of prostitute or debased social activity.
Thus, chu-hua were the feminine counterparts to chu-tzu.
See Kani Hiroaki, Kindai Chūgoku no kurī to "choka",[b]
pp. v-xiii. From the few chapters I have read of this
book, it looks like a major study of substantial interest
to a wide variety of scholars.

3. This essay was written originally in English.

Chapter 4.

1. Kusano Yasushi, "The Establishment of Topsoil
Practices"[b] (Hōbun ronsō 39 [1977]).

1a. Articulated further in his book, Chūgoku ni
okeru "kōsakken no kakuritsu" ki o meguru shomondai,
kyobō na gakumon dan'atsu ni taisuru fukutsu no kōsō
kiroku (Various problems surrounding the period of the
"establishment of cultivator rights" in China: A record
of indefatiguable resistance to intense academic pressure).[c]

2. See p. 176, n. 1 above.

3. See p. 176, n. 4 above.

4. See Hoshi, p. 409. According to Kusano, li-chia
chiao-tien was a "law" ensuring that one could freely
sell the land that one had developed up to the amount
one had invested in it. See Kusano, "The Reclamation
of Swamps and the Beginnings of a One-Field Two-Owners
System in the Sung and Yüan"[d] (Tōyō gakuhō 53.1-2 [1970]).

5. See Hoshi, p. 178.

6. What exactly ting-shou means will be the topic

of a later segment of Fujii's article.

6a. See also, Kusano, "The Reclamation of Swamps
and the Beginning of the One-Field Two-Owners System
in the Sung and Yüan,"[d] Tōyō gakuhō 53.1-2; Kusano,
"Topsoil Practice in Old China: The Material Base of
Topsoil and Various Legal and Customary Rights,"[e] Hōbun
ronsō 36 (1975); and Kusano, "Topsoil Practices in Old
China: Transfer of Control over the Topsoil and Cultivation Rights of Tenants,"[f] Tōyōshi kenkyū 34.2 (1972).

7. Chang Lü-hsiang (1611-74) withdrew from the
factional and warring parties at the end of the Ming and
beginning of the Ch'ing, in order to support his family.
He was an ardent opponent of Wang Yang-ming's philosophy
and an equally strong figure in the effort to revive
the work of Chu Hsi. He wrote a well-known work on
agriculture, Pu nung-shu or supplement to the agricultural handbook of Mr. Shen (see above pp. 1-3). Chang
lived in Tung-hsiang, Chia-hsing, Chekiang. See the
biography of him in A. Hummel, ed., Eminent Chinese of
the Ch'ing Period, pp. 45-46.

8. The Shui-li ying-t'ien fu was an office set up
in 1726 by the Yung-cheng Emperor to try to irrigate and
grow rice on land in the capital region. Farmers from
South China were invited to instruct local Northerners
in rice-cultivation methods. With the death of the
Yung-cheng Emperor, the project collapsed. See Huang
Pei, Autocracy at Work, pp. 238-40. Do not be misled
by Hoshi's entry on ying-t'ien (p. 16) which concerns
an earlier institution by the same name which was the
civilian equivalent of t'un-t'ien or military colonies.

9. A cursory reading of Hayashi's article indicates
that he is aware of the remarkable similarities of his
work with that of G. W. Skinner.

10. Tsao-li was originally a type of corvée demanded
of the peasantry by local officials in the Ming. Although

later replaced by ku-i, a payment in silver rather than
labor, poor peasants had no choice but to comply with
tsao-li. To do so, some became ya-i (yamen runners) for
local officials and were used by local inspectors to
gather information on the local gentry and li-chia
bosses. So, in the late Ming some ya-i became known as
wo-fang, specialists in digging up incriminating information. Wada argues that in their efficiency reports
they used this activity to exploit the local populace
on behalf of the local gentry. See especially his
article[e].

11. See Morohashi Tetsuji, Dai Kan-Wa jiten (The
great Sino-Japanese dictionary),[a] vol. 10, p. 740.

12. See ibid., vol. 7, p. 1132.

13. Kung-i were public meetings of landlords and
village functionaries to decide matters of interest to
the locality. Peasants, even if consulted, were only
present to facilitate cooperation when circumstances
required it. See Imahori Seiji, Chūgoku gendai shi
kenkyū josetsu (An introduction to the study of contemporary Chinese history),[a] p. 15; and Hoshi, p. 122.

Chapter 5.

1. "AF" is shorthand for the Asia Foundation which
was planning to fund the Tōyō bunko in the 1960's
(during the Vietnam War). It was considered dirty money
by many Japanese scholars because of its CIA links.
Ichiko Chūzō, head of the Modern China Section of the
Tōyō bunko, led the minority that wanted to accept the
money.

2. "Reproduction" (saiseisan) does not imply the
spawning of offspring. It is often used by Japanese
sinologists in its philosophical sense of the process
whereby something is recreated or caused to exist anew.
Here, public authority (focusing on the emperor) is

reproduced, albeit fleetingly, in the public servant or
local official. From a tenant's perspective, the magistrate is the representative of authority to which
the tenant may appeal.

3. A reference to the Russian terrorist group,
Narodnaya Volya (Will of the people), active at the end
of the 19th century. Their message elicited a certain
amount of appeal in early 20th century China as well.

4. Chien-tao was a stretch of land at the source
of the Yalu River on the Sino-Korean border. In the
late 19th century use of the land for agriculture had
stirred up conflict with Korean migrants. Japan became
embroiled in the dispute when Korea came under Japanese
control. In August 1907 Japan then claimed a good part
of it as Korean territory. Sung Chiao-jen investigated
the whole matter by infiltrating Japanese groups and
collecting documents in Korea. He subsequently wrote
a pamphlet entitled Chien-tao wen-t'i (The Chien-tao
question) to prove that the land was incontrovertably
Chinese. See K. C. Liew, Struggle for Democracy: Sung
Chiao-jen and the 1911 Revolution in China, pp. 65-67.

5. A usually scornful (but here ironic, even
facetious) reference to the postwar reassessment of
much of Japan's prewar output on Chinese history. Prewar
sinologists have often been attacked since 1945 for
providing an intellectual cosmetic for Japanese imperialist expansion onto the Asian mainland, such as the
popularization of the belief that China was stagnant
(history-less) until Japan came along and woke her up.
The problem, however, is that now the Chinese themselves
seem to be issuing their own self-critical "theory of
stagnation," which (coincidentally) fits well with the
Chinese Marxist interpretation of pre-foreign contact
theories. So, postwar Japanese scholarship on China is
really at some threshold.

6. "Saigo no rannā" in Japanese. Rannā is a base-
ball loan word referring to a runner on base.

Chapter 6.

1. Discussion of the first part of Oh's article
appears above, p. 74.

2. See summary above, p. 180, n. 13.

3. When Li Tzu-ch'eng took the city of Hsiang-yang
(Hupeh) in 1643, he changed its name to Hsiang-ching
and made it his capital. In the spring of 1644 he named
his kingdom Ta-shun, and later that year (April) he took
Peking. See his entry in Hummel, Eminent Chinese of
Ch'ing Period, p. 492.

4. The ten wealthiest households (within a total
of 110 households) in the li-chia system. Each year a
different li-chang was charged with collecting taxes.
See Hoshi, p. 406.

5. In the li-chia system the 100 households (ex-
cluding the ten li-chang) were divided into ten chia
who shared responsibility for providing a headman or
chia-shou. See Jerry Dennerline, "Fiscal Reform and
Local Reform," in Conflict and Control in Late Imperial
China, ed. Wakeman and Grant, p. 91.

6. In conjunction with changes in the li-chia
system, people were registered into occupational groups
(scholars, monks, etc.), one of which was for local officials: kuan-t'u. See Hoshi, zokuhen, p. 21.

7. "Official tithing," as described by Jerry
Dennerline, The Chia-ting Loyalists: Confucian Leadership and Social Change in Seventeenth-Century China, p.100.

8. This was a method of tax assessment based on
land rather than households that was used in the early
Ch'ing to correct for certain problems bequeathed by
the chün-t'ien chün-i system. Households were assigned

to mapped zones on which were plotted lands owned, graves,
and dikes. See Hoshi, zokuhen, p. 87.

9. A method of tax collection implemented to alle-
viate difficulties when a landowner's residence was
distant from his scattered holdings. For the tax
registers, all of one's lands were put together with
taxes assessed on the principal owners accordingly.
See Kuribayashi Nobuo, Rikōsei no kenkyū (A study of the
li-chia system),[b] pp. 340-46; and Hoshi, zokuhen, p. 87.

10. Land registers prepared by landowners with
drawings of assets in land. Since these drawings often
looked like fish scales, they were given the name yü-lin.

11. A local administrative unit in the Ch'ing just
smaller than the hsiang. See Hoshi, p. 314.

12. A local administrative unit in the Ch'ing just
smaller than the tu. See Hoshi, pp. 314, 316.

13. Hoshi, p. 413. Only landowners could become
liang-hu.

14. The assignment of tax collection beneath the
li-chang. See Hoshi, zokuhen, p. 59.

15. See Yamamoto Eiji, "Ming-Ch'ing Studies in Japan:
1976,"[b] Shigaku zasshi 86.5 (May 1977), pp. 204-205, for
a longer analysis of earlier work by Morita on i-t'u.

16. See the detailed discussion of this issue above
pp. 64-65.

17. For a brief discussion of this "illegal" practice,
see Niida's work (cited p. 176, n. 2 above), pp. 336-37,
350; and Hoshi, p. 6.

18. Discussion of these two items is considerably
fuller above pp. 58-66 and p. 176, n. 1.

19. See Hoshi, p. 311.

20. The Ming official in charge of local tax collec-

tion and transport of the tax monies. See Hoshi, p. 414
for much detail. Ray Huang calls them "tax captains,"
in Taxation and Government Finance in Sixteenth-Century
Ming China, p. 36.

21. A method of cultivating wetlands, used in
Szechwan, discussed by Chang Tsung-fa in the Ch'ing.
See Hoshi, p. 204.

22. An alternate name for the "guards" or wei (in
the wei-so system) that the Yung-lo Emperor used for
his wei outside the capital. See Albert Chan, The
Glory and Fall of the Ming Dynasty, p. 45.

23. My reading of Shiga's essay leads me to precisely
the opposite conclusion: that few codified laws were
employed in local litigation of civil cases.

Chapter 7.

1. "Ch'üan-shih liang-yen" was the name of the pamphlet by Liang A-fa that exerted such a strong influence
on Hung Hsiu-ch'uan.

2. See pp. 110-11, and p. 183, n. 15. I-t'u was a
form of rotational collection of the land tax by local
households for delivery to the magistrate in lieu of
collection by the yamen sub-bureaucracy.

3. See above p. 181, n. 3.

4. Kuo-lu-yin: literally, "transfer money." For the
necessary circulation of commodities in the Ying-k'ou
area, a need arose for a trading system that would reduce reliance on the use of copper coins and silver.
This led to the use of long-term credit transactions on
a barter basis by money-lenders, a system known as
kuo-lu-yin. It was a unique financial system, extremely
important in the developing trade and industry in Ying-
k'ou.

Chapter 8.

1. For an explanation of this term as used by Japanese sinologists, see above pp. 180-81, n. 2.

2. See above pp. 12-13.

3. See above p. 106.

4. In his essay Inoue points out that the historical records for Kwangtung speak of at least four kinds of bandits (tsei). T'u-tsei appears to be a generic term for local bandits, regardless of time. She-tsei, on the other hand, is a term that appears only for the late Ming and early Ch'ing in Kwangtung, and the she element, he argues, refers to the perceived "communal" or "social" nature of their organization. His point is to note that she-tsei revolts were not simply risings by nu-p'u but included other lower strata of the agrarian populace.

5. For a discussion of nu-pien, see p. 177, n. 9.

6. See above pp. 32-33 for a discussion of one of these essays. Her article[a] was translated into English: "On the Fluctuation of the Price of Rice in the Chiangnan Region during the First Half of the Ch'ing," Memoirs of the Research Department of the Toyo Bunko 37 (1979).

7. For a brief discussion of the work and school of Professor Ōtsuka Hisao, see Takeshi Ishida, "A Current Japanese Interpretation of Max Weber," The Developing Economies IV.3 (Sept. 1966), pp. 275-98.

8. One point of destination would be Immanual Wallerstein's "world systems" (author's note).

9. On li-chang, see above p. 182, n. 4.

10. Satō Kimihiko has shown how a single concept can simultaneously fuel both rebels and defenders of the establishment: "An Analysis of the Rebellion of the Ch'ing-shui Sect of Wang Lun in 1774: An Introduction

to a Theory of the Boxers,"[a] Hitotsubashi ronsō 81.3
(1979). See above p. 35 for a brief dicussion of this
essay.

11. Five notorious cases in which the Ming founder
purged thousands of landlords, many of whom had
earlier supported him fervently.

12. See above p. 179, n. 7.

Chapter 9.

1. Three work stoppages of June 9, 10, and 11 in
Shanghai in which workers held mass demonstrations in
support of the movement and against the government.

2. See above p. 182, n. 4. The three levels of
the t'u-chia system were tsung-hu (corresponding to the
li-chang under the li-chia system), tzu-hu (individual
families), and chao (a kind of servant).

3. "Minshūshi" or "history of the people" is a
relatively new enterprise among younger Japanese
historians of their own history, aimed as coming to a
better understanding of popular culture by using a
wide variety of sources and methods. It is also part
of an attack on the more established Marxism of their
Tokyo University elders. See Carol Gluck's illuminating
article: "The People in History: Recent Trends in
Japanese Historiography," Journal of Asian Studies 38.1
(Nov. 1978), pp. 25-50.

ARTICLES CITED

(Alphabetical by author)

ABE Hiroshi 阿部洋
a. 日本の「対支文化事業」と中国教育文化界 :
一九三〇年代後半期を中心として　52

ABE Seiji 阿部誠士
a. ロシアの極東政策と樺太久春古丹占拠　50

ADACHI Keiji 足立啓二　21
a. 明末清初の一農業経営 :「沈氏農書」の再
評価　3-5
b. 大豆粕流通と清代の商業的農業　4, 5-6, 43-44
c. 清代華北の農業経営と社会構造　113-14

AJIOKA Tōru 味岡徹
a. 第一次大戦初期の中国民族運動 : 二十ヵ
要求と中国民衆　48

AKASHI Iwao 明石岩雄
a. 新四国借款団に関する一考察 : ワシント冷議
にいたる列強と中国民族運動の対抗　48

AMANO Motonosuke 天野元之助　6

AOYAMA Jirō 青山次郎
a. 明代嘉靖朝の京営について　72

ARAKI Kengo 荒木見悟
a. 明末宗教思想研究管東溟の生涯とその
思想　38

ARITA Kazuo 有田和夫
a. 清末意議構造論のための試論　93
b.「翼教叢編」考　128
ASAI Motoi 浅井紀　101
a. 明末徐鴻儒の乱について　17

Aichi kyōiku daigaku kenkyū hōkoku-shakai kagaku
愛知教育大学研究報告-社会科学

Ajia keizai アジア経済

Ajia kenkyū アジア研究

Aoyama shigaku 青山史学

Atarashii rekishigaku no tame ni
新しい歴史学のために

Bunkei ronsō 文経論叢

Chiiki bunka kenkyū 地域文化研究

Chikaki ni arite (Kin-gendai Chūgoku o meguru tōron no hiroba) 近きに在りて（近現代中国をめぐる討論のひろば）

Chūgoku kenkyū geppō 中国研究月報

Chūgoku shi kenkyū, Ōsaka shiritsu daigaku
中国史研究 大阪市立大学

Chūgoku kindaishi kenkyū 中国近代史研究

Chūgoku kindaishi kenkyū tsūshin
中国近代史研究通信

Chūgoku shisō shi kenkyū 中国思想史研究

Chūgoku suiri shi kenkyū 中国水利史研究

Chung-kuo she-hui ching-chi shih yen-chiu
中国社会経済史研究

Chung-kuo shih yen-chiu tung-t'ai 中国史研究動態

Chūō daigaku bungakubu kiyō-Shigakka 中央大学文学部
紀要-史学科

Fukuoka joshi tandai kiyō 福岡女子短大紀要

Fukuoka kyōiku daigaku kiyō 福岡教育大学紀要

Gakujutsu kokusai kōryū sankō shiryōshū, Meiji University
学術国際交流参考資料集、明治

Gakushūin shigaku 学習院史学

Gunji shigaku 軍事史学

Handai hōgaku 阪大法学

Hiroshima daigaku Tōyōshi kenkyūshitsu hōkoku
広島大学東洋史研究室報告

Hisutoria ヒストリア

Hitotsubashi ronsō 一橋論叢

Hōbun ronsō 法文論叢

Hōgaku kenkyū, Hokkai gakuen daigaku hōgakkai
法学研, 北海学園大学法学会

Hokkaidō daigaku bungakubu kiyō
北海島大学文学部紀要

Hokkaidō daigaku jimbun kagaku ronshū
北海島大学人文科学論集

Hōsei ronshū 法政論集

Jimbun, Kyōto daigaku kyōyōbu 人文, 京都大学教養部

Jimbun kagaku ronshū 人文科学論集

Jimbun ronkyū, Kansai Gakuin University
人文論究, 関西学院

Kagoshima keidai ronshū 鹿児島経大論集

Kaigai jijō 海外事情

Kaiji shi kenkyū 海事史研究

Kan 韓

Kanazawa daigaku bungaku ronshū-shigakka hen
金沢大学文学部論集-史学科編

Keiō gijuku daigaku gengo bunka kenkyūjo kiyō
慶応義塾大学言語文化研究所紀要

Keizaigaku ronshū 経済学論集

Keizai keiei ronsō 経済経営論叢

Kikan jinruigaku 季刊人類学

Kindai Chūgoku 近代中国

Kinyū keizai 金融経済

Kita Kyūshū daigaku gakubu kiyō
北九州大学学部紀要

Kōchi kōgyō kōtō senmon gakkō gakujutsu kiyō
高知工業高等専門学校学術紀

Kokka gakkai zasshi 国家学会雑誌

Kokugakuin daigaku kiyō 国学院大学紀要

Kokusai kankeigaku kenkyū, Tsūdajuku daigaku kiyō
国際関係学研究, 津田塾大学紀要

Kumamoto daigaku bungakubu ronsō-shigaku hen
熊本大学文学部論叢-史学編

Kumamoto daigaku kyōiku gakubu kiyō
熊本大学教育学部紀要

Kumamoto daigaku kyōiku gakubu kiyō-Jimbun kagaku
熊本大学教育学部紀要-人文科学

Kumatsu shū 响沫集

Kyūshū daigaku Tōyōshi ronshū 九州大学東洋史論集

Li-shih yen-chiu 歴史研究

Mindaishi kenkyū 明代史研究

Minzokugaku kenkyū 民族学研究

Nagoya daigaku bungakubu kenkyū kiyō ronshū
名古屋大学文学部研究紀要論集

Nagoya daigaku Tōyōshi kenkyū hōkoku
名古屋大学東洋史研究報告

Nagoya gakuin daigaku ronshū-shakai kagaku hen
名古屋学院大学論集・社会科学編

Nihon Chūgoku gakkaihō 日本中国学会報

Nihon rekishi 日本歴史

Nihon shi kenkyū 日本史研究

Ochanomizu shigaku お茶の水史学

Ōita daigaku kyōiku gakubu kenkyū kiyō-Jimbun shakai kagaku 大分大学教育学部研究紀要-人文社会科学

Okayama daigaku hōgakkai zasshi 岡山大学法学会雑誌

Ōsaka daigaku bungakubu kyōdō kenkyū ronshū 大阪大学文学部共同研究論集

Ōsaka daigaku kyōyōbu kenkyū shūroku-Jimbun shakai kagaku 大阪大学教養部研究集録-人文社会科学

Ōsaka kyōiku daigaku kiyō 大阪教育大学紀要

Rekishigaku kenkyū 歴史学研究

Rekishigaku no saiken ni mukete 歴史学の再建に向けて

Rekishi hyōron 歴史評論

Rekishi jinrui 歴史人類

Rekishi kenkyū, Aichi Kyōiku University 歴史研究, 愛知教育

Rekishi to bunka, Iwate University 歴史と文化, 岩手

Rekishi to bunka, Tōkyō daigaku kyōyōbu 歴史と文化, 東京大学教育部

Rikkyō hōgaku 立教法学

Ritsumeikan bungaku 立命館文学

Ritsumeikan hōgaku 立命館法学

Ritsumeikan shigaku 立命館史学

Ryūkoku shidan 龍谷史壇

Seiji keizai shigaku 政治経済史学

Seishin joshi daigaku ronsō 聖心女子大学論叢

Seiyō shigaku　西洋史学

Senshū shigaku　専修史学

Shakai bunka shigaku　社会文化史学

Shakai kagaku jānaru　社会科学ジャーナル

Shakai kagaku kenkyū, Tōkyō daigaku shakai kagaku kenkyūjo
社会科学研究, 東京大学社会科学研究所

Shakai keizai shigaku　社会経済史学

Shichō　史潮

Shien　史淵

Shien, Rikkyō daigaku shigakkai
史苑, 立教大学史学会

Shigaku　史学

Shigaku kenkyū　史学研究

Shigaku zasshi　史学雑誌

Shihō　史朋

Shikan　史観

Shimane daigaku hōbungakubu kiyō
島根大学法文学部紀要

Shingai kakumei kenkyū　辛亥革命研究

Shinshū daigaku jimbun kagaku ronshū
信州大学人文科学論集

Shirin　史林

Shiron　史論

Shisei　史正

Shisō　思想

Shisō*　史抄

Shisō, Nihon daigaku shigakka 史叢, 日本大学史学科

Shūkan Tōyōgaku　集刊東洋学

Sundai shigaku 駿台史学

Takushoku daigaku ronshū 拓殖大学論集

Tetsugaku nempō 哲学年報

Tenri daigaku gakuhō 天理大学学報

Tō-A keizai kenkyū 東亜経済研究

Tochi seido shigaku 土地制度史学

Tōdaishi kenkyūkai hōkoku 唐代史研究会報告

Tōhōgaku 東方学

Tōhō gakuhō 東方学報

Tōhoku gakuin daigaku ronshū-Rekishigaku chirigaku
東北学院大学論集-歴史学地理学

Tōkai daigaku bungakubu kiyō 東海大学文学部紀要

Tōkyō daigaku kyōyō gakubu jimbun kagakka kiyō
東京大学教養学部人文科学科紀要

Tōkyō gaikokugo daigaku ronshū 東京外国語大学論集

Tōkyō gakugei daigaku kiyō-Jimbun kagaku
東京学芸大学紀要-人文科学

Tōkyō joshi daigaku ronshū 東京女子大学論集

Toyama daigaku jimbun gakubu kiyō
富山大学人文学部紀要

Tōyō bunka 東洋文化

Tōyō bunka kenkyūjo kiyō 東洋文化研究所紀要

Tōyō bunko shohō 東洋文庫書報

Tōyō gakuhō 東洋学報

Tōyōgaku ronsō--Tōyō daigaku bungakubu kiyō, Bukkyō gakka,
Chūgoku tetsugaku bungakka hen 東洋学論叢-
東洋大学文学部紀要,仏教学科,中国哲学文学科編

Tōyōshi kenkyū 東洋史研究

Tōyōshi ron 東洋史論

Utsunomiya daigaku kyōiku gakubu kiyō

宇都宮大学教育学部紀要

Yamagata daigaku kiyō 山形大学紀要

Yamaguchi daigaku bungakkaishi

山口大学文学会誌.

Yasuda gakuen kenkyū kiyō 安田学園研究紀要

Yokohama shiritsu daigaku ronsō-Jimbun kagaku keiretsu

横浜市立大学論叢-人文科学系列

BOOKS AND COLLECTIONS OF ESSAYS

(All publishers located in Tokyo unless otherwise noted)

<u>Ajia gendaishi I: Teikoku shugi no jidai</u>
アジア現代史Ⅰ: 帝国主義の時代　 (Aoki shoten).

<u>Ajia gendaishi II: Minzoku undō no hatten no jidai</u>
アジア現代史Ⅱ: 民族運動の発展の時代 (Aoki shoten).

<u>Chiiki shakai no shiten</u>:

<u>Chiiki shakai no shiten:Chiiki shakai to riidā</u>
地域社会の視点: 地域 社会とリーダー　, ed. Dept.
of East Asian History, Faculty of Letters, Nagoya
University, Nagoya.

<u>Chūgoku minshū hanran shi</u> 中国民衆叛乱史
(History of popular uprisings in China), ed. Tanigawa
Michio 谷川道雄　and Mori Masao 森正夫　(Heibonsha):
Part 2: <u>Sō-Min chūki</u> 宋・明中期　 (Sung to mid-Ming);
Part 3: <u>Minmatsu-Shin</u> 明末・清　(Late Ming and Ch'ing).

<u>Gendai rekishigaku no seika to kadai</u> 現代歴史学
の成果と課題 (Achievements and topics in contemporary historiography), ed. Rekishigaku kenkyūkai.

<u>Goshi undō no kenkyū</u> 五四運動の研究 (Studies on
the May Fourth Movement), Kyoto, Dōhōsha.

<u>Hoshi ronshū</u>:

<u>Hoshi hakushi taikan kinen Chūgoku shi ronshū</u> 星博士
退官記念中国史論集　 (Essays in Chinese
history in commeroation of the retirement of Professor
Hoshi Ayao), Yamagata University.

<u>Kaga ronshū</u>:

<u>Kaga hakushi taikan kinen: Chūgoku bunshitetsugaku ronshū</u>
加賀博士退官記念: 中国文史哲学論集
(Essays in Chinese literature, history, and philosophy

in commemoration of the retirement of Professor Kaga),
Kōdansha.

Kenryōku kōzō:

Chūgoku ni okeru kenryoku kōzō no shiteki kenkyū 中国
における権力構造の史的研究　(Historical studies
of the power structure in China), ed. Imanaga Seiji
今永清二 , Hiroshima.

Kindai Nihon to Higashi Ajia 近代日本と東アジア
(Yamakawa shuppansha, annual report of the Kindai
Nihon kenkyūkai).

Kinsei toshi no hikaku shiteki kenkyū 近世都市の
比較史的研究 (no publication information available).

Kōza:

Kōza: Chūgoku kin-gendaishi 講座：中国近現代史
(Symposium on modern and contemporary Chinese history),
Tokyo University Press).

Ming-Ch'ing shih kuo-chi hsüeh-shu t'ao-lun-hui lun-wen-
chi 明清史国際学術討論会論文集 (Essays
for the International Academic Symposium on Ming and
Ch'ing History, Tientsin).

Mori ronshū:

Mori Mikisaburō hakushi shōju kinen: Tōyōgaku ronshū
森三樹三郎博士頌寿記念：東洋学論集
(Essays in East Asian studies in honor of Professor
Mori Mikisaburō), Meiyū shoten.

Nagoya ronshū:

Nagoya daigaku bungakubu sanjū shūnen kinen ronshū
名古屋大学文学部三十周年記念論集
(Essays commemorating the 30th anniversary of the
Faculty of Letters, Nagoya University), Nagoya.

Nakajima ronshū:

Nakajima Satoshi sensei koki kinen ronshū 中嶋敏
先生古稀記念論集 (Essays commemorating the
70th birthday of Professor Nakajima), Kyūko shoin, 2 vols.

Nakayama ronsō:

Nakayama Hachirō kyōju shōju kinen: Min-Shin shi ronsō

中山八郎教授頌寿記念：明清史論叢
(Essays in Ming and Ch'ing history in honor of
Professor Nakayama Hachirō), Ryōgen shoten.

Namae ronshū:

Rekishi ronshū: Namae Yoshio sensei kanreki kinen

歴史論集：生江義男先生還暦記念. (Historical
essays in commemoration of the 61st birthday of
Professor Namae Yoshio).

Nihon teikoku shugi to Higashi Ajia 日本帝国主義
と東アジア , ed. Kojima Reiitsu 小島麗逸 (Ajia
keizai kenkyūjo).

Nitchū kankei to bunka masatsu 日中関係と文化
摩擦 (Sino-Japanese relations and cultural friction),
ed. Abe Hiroshi 阿部洋 , Gannandō.

Ono ronshū:

Ono Katsutoshi hakushi shōju kinen Tōhōgaku ronshū

小野勝年博士頌寿記念東方学論集
(Essays in East Asian studies in honor of Professor
Ono Katsutoshi), Kyoto, Ryūkoku University Research
Group on East Asian History.

Rekishi kagaku:

Rekishi kagaku taikei XIV: Ajia no henkaku 歴史
科学大系 XIV：アジアの変改 (Historical science
series XIV: Reforms in Asia), Azekura shobō.

Sakai ronshū:

Rekishi ni okeru minshū to bunka: Sakai Tadao sensei
koki shukuga kinen ronshū 歴史における民衆と
文化：酒井忠夫先生古稀祝賀記念.
(People and culture in history: Essays commemorating
the 70th birthday of Professor Sakai Tadao), Kokusho
kankōkai.

Satō ronshū:
Satō hakushi kanreki kinen Chūgoku suiri shi ronshū
佐藤博士還暦記念、中国水利史論集
(Essays on the history of water conservancy in China,
commemorating the 61st birthday of Professor Satō),
Kokusho kankōkai.

Shigaku ronsō:
Shigaku kenkyū gojū shūnen kinen ronsō 史学研究
五十周年記念論叢 (Essays commemorating the
50th anniversity of Shigaku kenkyū), "sekai hen"
世界編 (international section), ed. Hiroshima
shigaku kenkyūkai 広島史学研究会

Shingai hōkoku:
Shingai kakumei shichijū shūnen kinen Tōkyō kokusai
gakujutsu kaigi hōkoku 辛亥革命七十周年
記念東京国際学術会議報告 (Report of the
Tokyo International Scholarly Conference Commemorating
the 70th Anniversay of the 1911 Revolution).

Taiwan kin-gendaishi kenkyū 台湾近現代史研究
(Ryōkei shosha).

Uchida ronshū:
Tōyōshi ronshū: Uchida Gimpū hakushi shōju kinen
東洋史論集：内田吟風博士頌寿記念.
(Essays in East Asian history in honor of Professor
Uchida Gimpū), Kyoto, Dōhōsha.

ADDENDUM

Ichiko ronshū:
Ronshū kindai Chūgoku kenkyū: Ichiko kyōju taikan kinen
ronsō 論集近代中国研究：市古教授退官
記念論叢 (Essays on modern China in honor of the
retirement of Professor Ichiko), Yamakawa shuppansha.

Chan Jo-shui 湛若水

Chang Chien 張謇

Chang-chou fu-chih 漳州府志

Chang Lü-hsiang 張履祥

Chang Nien-i 張念一

Chang Ping-lin 章炳麟

Chang Tsung-fa 張宗法

Ch'ang-p'ing 昌平

chao 爪

chao-t'ien 照天

che-liang-yin 析糧銀

Ch'en-ch'üeh chi 陳確集

Ch'en Lung-cheng 陳龍正

ch'eng-chia 承価

Chi 薊

Ch'i-chen chi-wen lu 啟禎記聞錄

ch'i-chuang-hu 寄莊戶

Ch'i-shan 琦善

ch'i-su 耆宿

chia 甲

chia-cheng 甲正

chia-shou 甲首

chiang-ling 捭領

chiao-an 教案

Chiao Hsün 焦循

Chiao-min pang-wen 教民榜文

chieh-mei-kuan 姊妹館

chieh-sheng 節省

chien-chia shui 間架稅

chien-ch'üan 繭捐

Chien-ch'ün li-lüeh 監軍曆略

chien-hang 繭行

chien-sheng 監生

Chien-tao wen-t'i 間島問題

Ch'ien I-pen 錢一本

"Ch'ien-liang lun" 錢糧論

Ch'ien-lung K'un-shan Hsin-yang ho-chih 乾隆崑山新陽合志

chien shakai 地緣社会

chih 賀

chiiki shakai 地域社会

chin 金

chin-shih 進士

ching-shih chi-min 経世済民

ch'ing 情

ch'ing-li 情理

Ch'ing-liu-p'ai 清流派

Ch'ing-shih kao 清史稿

Ch'ing-shih lun-ts'ung 清史論叢

ch'iu 坵

Chou Hsüeh-hsi 周学熙

Ch'ou-hai t'u-pien 籌海図編

Chu Hsi 朱熹

chu-hua 豬花

chu-tzu 豬仔

Chu Yüan-chang 朱元璋

chuan-chih 転質

Ch'uan-pi 川鼻

chun-t'ien 准田

Chung-ho-t'ang 中和堂

Chung-hua min-kuo kung-chin hui 中華民国共進会

chung-jen 中人

chung-teng she-hui 中等社会

Ch'ung-ming hsien-chih 崇明県志

Ch'uo-keng lu 輟耕録

chü-jen 挙人

chün 均

chün-t'ien chün-i 均田均役

ch'ün 羣

fa 法

Fan Chung-yen 范仲淹

fang-hsing 訪行

fang-ku 房股

fen-chih-t'ien 糞質田

feng-su 風俗

fu-nung 富農

Hakka 客家

Hsi-hsi hung-chün 西系紅軍

hao-ch'iang 豪強

hao-nu 豪奴

Hsi-yu chi 西遊記

hsia-hu 下戸

hsiang-lao 郷老

hsin-hsüeh 心学

hsiang 郷

hsiang-hsien 郷賢

hsiang-pao 郷保

hsiang-shen 郷紳

hsiang-yüeh 郷約

hsien-k'e-i 減科議

hsing-ling 性霊

Hsiu-chu yü-t'an shih-i
修築圩坦事宣
hsü-li 胥吏
Hsü Shou-hui 徐壽輝
hsüan-chiang 宣講
hsüan-chüan 宣卷
Hsüan-fu 宣府
hsün-ch'en 勳臣
hu 戶
huan-p'i 換批
Huang Hsing 黃興
Huang Ju-ch'eng 黃汝成
huang-ts'e 黃冊
Huang Tsung-hsi 黃宗羲
Hung Hsiu-ch'uan 洪秀全
i-ch'an liang-chia
一產兩価
"I-ch'ien wei-fu"
从錢為賦
i-lang 議榔
I-men 義門
I-nien ho-shang 一念和尚
Isshinkai 一進会
i-t'ai 从太
i-t'u 義図
Jih-chih lu 日知錄
kai-hu 丐戶

Kan-hsiang 甘泉
Kan Tzu-chieh 甘子价
k'ao-cheng 考証
k'ao-yü 考語
Keng Chü 耿橘
kenryoku shikō kei
權力志向型
ketsuen shakai
血緣社会
Koike Chōzō 小池張造
Ko-lao-hui 哥老会
k'o-hu 客戶
k'o-kang 客綱
k'o-min 客民
Ku Hsien-ch'eng 顧憲成
ku-i 顧役
Ku Yen-wu 顧炎武
kuan-chia 官甲
kuan-ch'ien-chü 官錢局
kuan-ch'ien-piao 官錢票
kuan-p'ing 官評
kuan-shang 官商
kuan-shih 管事
Kuan-t'ien shih-mo k'ao
官田始末考
kuan-t'u 官図
Kuang-fu hui 光復会

kui-chi 詭寄

kung 公

kung-i 公議

kung-sang chü 公桑局

kung-sheng 貢生

K'ung Yin 空印

kuo-chia chu-i 国家主義

kuo-chung chih ch'ien
過種之錢

Kuo Huan 郭桓

kuo-lu-yin 過爐銀

kuo-min 国民

kuo-t'ou 過投

kuo-t'ou-yin 過投銀

kyōdōtai 共同体

kyōshin ron 郷紳論

kyōshin shihai 郷紳支配

kyōson iji kei
郷村維持型

li 理

li-chang 里長

li-chia 里甲

li-chia chiao-tien
立価交佃

Li Chih 李贄

Li Hung-chang 李鴻章

li-lao 里老

li-lao-jen 里老人

Li-p'ai kung-chu chih
里排公築制

Li San-ts'ai 李三才

Li-shih yen-chiu 歷史研究

Li Tzu-ch'eng 李自成

Liang A-fa 梁阿發

liang-chang 糧長

Liang Ch'i-ch'ao 梁啓超

liang-hu 糧戶

Lien-chuang hui 聯莊会

lien-yü chieh-chia
連圩結甲

ling-hu ts'e 另戶冊

Liu I-shun 劉義順

Lo Ju-fang 羅汝芳

Lung-kan hsien-chih
龍巖県志

Lü K'un 呂坤

mai-chia 買価

min-chih chu-i 民治主義

mien-kuei sha-chien
綿貴紗賤

min-pien 民弁

Ming-i tai-fang lu
明夷待訪録

Ming-shih 明史

Ming-shih chi-shih pen-mo
明史紀事本末

Ming T'ai-tsu 明太祖

minshūshi 民衆史

Mitsui 三井

Miu Tzu 繆梓

Mori Kaku 森恪

nan-liang pei-tiao
南糧北調

nan-shui pei-tiao
南水北調

Nguyễn 阮

nu-pien 奴変

nu-p'u 奴僕

nü-kuan 女館

nü-ying 女営

pa-t'ou 把頭

pai-lien-chiao 白蓮教

pan-ch'eng-chia 半承価

pan-chün 班軍

pan-t'u 版図

pao-chia 保甲

Pao-chüan 宝巻

Pao-ting 保定

Pei-hsi-hsing 北四行

p'ei-pen 培本

pu-cheng shih-ssu 布政使司

Pu nung-shu 補農書

p'u 舗

punti 本地

rannā ランナー

rieki tsuikyū kei
利益追求型

saiseisan 再生産

seikatsu kyōdōtai
生活共同体

shang 商

Shang-ch'eng hsien-chih
商成県志

shang-hu 上戸

shang-ku 商股

shang-nung 上農

Shang-shu yin-i 尚書引義

she-chi 社稷

she-tsei 社賊

shen 紳

shen-chin 紳衿

shen-nü 神女

shen-shih 紳士

sheng-kuan fa-ts'ai 昇官発財

Sheng-tse chen 盛沢鎮

Sheng-yen-hui 聖言会

sheng-yüan 生員

shih 士

shih-jen 士人

shih-shih ch'iu-shih 実事求是

"Shih-yüan chieh-yin" 釋怨結姻

Shuang-huai sui-ch'ao 雙槐歲鈔

Shui-hu chuan 水滸伝

Shui-li ying-t'ien fu 水利営田府

shun-chuang 順莊

so-ch'ou ch'ien 所酬銭

Soong Chia-shu 宋嘉樹

soyaku kōkan 租約更換

"Su-Sung erh-fu t'ien-fu chih chung" 蘇松二府田賦之重

suiri kyōdōtai 水利共同体

Sun Ting-ch'en 孫鼎臣

ssu 私

ssu-hsiang chieh-fang 思想解放

Sung Chiao-jen 宋教仁

ta-hang 打行

Ta Ming pao-ch'ao 大明宝鈔

"Ta-tan lun" 韃靼論

Tachibna shiraki 98

T'an Ssu-t'ung 譚嗣同

tang-i 当役

tao 道

Tao-ch'ing chen-chih 島清鎮志

T'ao Hsü 陶煦

T'ao Tsung-i 陶宗儀

ti-fang 地方

ti-fang kung-cheng shen-ch'i 地方公正紳耆

ti-fang shih-shen 地方士紳

ti-pao 地保

ti-ting-yin 地丁銀

t'ieh-i 貼役

t'ieh-ta 鉄搭

tien-li 佃力

t'ien-ping 田兵

t'ien-t'ou 田頭

t'ien-tsei 田賊

ting 丁

ting-li 定理

Ting Lü-heng 丁履恒

ting-shou 頂首

T'ing-lin wen-chi 亭林文集

t'ing-sung 聽訟

t'ou-sheng-yin 投生銀

Ts'ai Yüan-p'ei 蔡元培

ts'an-sang chü 蠶桑局

tsao-li 皂隸

tsei 賊

Tseng Kuo-fan 曾国藩

Tso Tsung-t'ang 左宗棠

tsu-chan 租棧

tsu-ku 租股

tsu-t'ien 租田

ts'ui-pan 催辦

tsung-hu 総戶

tu 都

t'u 図

t'u-chia 図甲

t'u-hao 土豪

t'u-t'ou 図頭

t'u-tsei 土賊

t'un-t'ien 屯田

Tung-lin 東林

T'ung-meng-hui 同盟会

T'ung-shan hui 同善会

t'ung-yüan 銅元

tzu-hu 子戶

tzu-p'ei 資賠

Uchida Ryōhei 内田良平

wan-tien 頑佃

Wang Ken 王艮

Wang-ts'ai Huang-Ming t'ai-hsüeh chih
工材皇明太学志.

Wang Yang-ming 王陽明

Wei-hsüan-fu 衛選簿

Wei Li Wei Chi-tzu wen-chi
魏礼·魏季子文集

wei-so 衛所

wen 文

Wen-sheng 文賸

wu-lai 無賴

Wu Liang 吳亭

wu-shan wu-o 無善無悪

ya-chin 押金

ya-i 衙役

ya-tsu 押租

ya-tsu-t'ien 押租田

Yang Tseng-hsin 楊增新

Yang Tu-sheng 楊篤生

yang-wu 洋務

yao 繇

yao-t'ieh 繇帖

yeh-shih 業食

"Yin-Chou chih-tu lun"
殷周制度論

ying-chün 営軍

yu-mien 優免

yu-t'ieh 由帖

yu-ts'un 郵村

yü-lin 魚鱗

Yü-lin 楡林   Yüan Shih-k'ai 袁世凱

Yüan 袁   yü-t'ou 圩頭

Yüan-shih 元史   Yün Tai-ying 惲代英

CM/CJ annotated biblio — C eco hist. 88